ADVENTURES OF A TRACTOR BOY

Adventures of a
Tractor Boy

GRAEME BROOKE

tractor press

Published by tractor press

ISBN-13: 978-1499350579

ISBN-10: 1499350570

DEDICATION

This book is dedicated to my long suffering wife Sharon, and to my daughters, Rachel and Leah, who are carrying on the tradition of following the Tractor Boys too.

Additionally, I would like to dedicate this book to two of my friends who died at an early age, Nick Coppin who went to many away games with me and Matthew Page, a Wolves fan who attended many games with me between the sides.

I would also like to mention Pat Edwards and Jill Lewis of the Clacton Branch whose dedication and organisation over the years has meant the ability to travel to many games for supporters based in Essex, particularly long away trips for night matches which might not have been possible otherwise. This has now been taken on to a lesser degree in recent years by Rita Mackenzie and the Manningtree Branch.

CONTENTS

INTRODUCTION

Were you the kid who grew up so immersed in football it impacted your whole life? Are you close to someone whose life is dominated by the love of a particular football team and do you wonder why? If you'd like to understand this strange obsession, or maybe share the experiences of a fellow-sufferer, read this real-life adventure of an extreme fan who has followed his team through thick and thin. It doesn't matter which team you follow, the dedication and irrational behaviour will always be the same.

Whilst on European tours, he's played football in the street with Paul Mariner, posed as a Town player at the player's hotel, been hunted by a wolf in Norway, had a snowball fight whilst on a European Tour in August, led a gang of naked supporters chasing Dutch Car Thieves, had a drinking session with Hindus in Copenhagen, been a reporter for Radio Orwell, had bottles thrown at him whilst singing God Save the Queen to St Etienne supporters, helped clothe a Liverpool Supporter on a boat train in Germany and been to the San Siro with Marcus Stewart's other half.

At home, the adventures continued including driving a minibus to Sunderland dressed as a Gorilla, hidden from Millwall fans in a

Ladies toilets, had a ride in a Black Maria from Goodison to escape angry scousers, visiting 15 pubs on a tour of the Peak District on the way home from a 5-0 defeat at Anfield, been in a police car chase, stayed sober on New Year's Eve so he could see Town at Port Vale (and lose 5-0!), got Jimmy Hill to say something nice about Ipswich and been sick on Frank McClintock. Also, he explains his hatred for Villa Park and how he missed out on his vow to watch Town at Anfield until they won!

Graeme Brooke won the SuperFan competition in 1984 in recognition of his dedication in the late 70s and early 80s and attended his 1000th match against Norwich in 2002. Although still an ardent season ticket holder he currently cannot get to as many away games as previously as often occurs with family commitments. He likes to attend the more insane away games such as Leeds or Yeovil on a Tuesday night. He is married with 18 year old and 8 year old daughters and lives in Mistley in Essex.

These are just some of the crazy antics of a Tractor Boy. This is a book that should not only appeal to other Tractor Boys and Girls but should appeal to any football supporter, particularly those that remember the 70s and 80s. It will also appeal to those of you not particularly into football but that have a passion or dedication that you will go to extraordinary lengths to partake in.

CHAPTER 1

THE EARLY DAYS AND HOW IT ALL STARTED

Were you the kid who grew up so immersed in football it impacted your whole life? Are you close to someone whose life is dominated by the love of a particular football team and do you wonder why? If you'd like to understand this strange obsession, or maybe share the experiences of a fellow-sufferer, read this real-life adventure of an extreme fan who has followed his team through thick and thin. It doesn't matter which team you follow, the dedication and irrational behaviour will always be the same.

A question I have often asked myself (particularly during the lows) was how and why I have watched over a 1000 Ipswich games?

How did I start and was it love at first sight?

It all started with my first ever Ipswich game on 8th March 1975. It was the FA Cup epic, which went over four matches starting with a home game to Leeds United. (It was in the days when there was no limitation on the number of replays played.)

Prior to this I had actually been a follower of Leeds United. Let me explain; in my view a follower is someone who never goes to watch a team that they like but watches them on television, listens to them on the radio and reads all the newspaper articles – a really dedicated follower may also buy the team kit (you know the type – a typical Manchester United follower that has never been within 200 miles of Old Trafford). That was what I was with Leeds United but I did have an excuse – my age of 11 at the time made it difficult to attend matches even though my family hailed from that part of the country. Anyway, when Brian Clough joined Leeds United, that put me right off them (I cannot recall why I did not like him) so I decided to look for a team that I could not only be a follower but a supporter (someone who actually went and watched their team play). Even though Clough was only at Leeds United for 43 days, I was never tempted back, although I still have a bit of a soft spot for them.

Who could I support? Well being a young lad of 11 with limited monies, the choice was narrowed down immediately to either Ipswich Town or Colchester United.

Although I do follow the U's results, I had left myself the choice between my two local teams, one in the top flight and one in the lower regions of the football league so it was an easy choice to make and I have supported Ipswich Town (now known as the Tractor Boys) since that day in March 1975.

The build up to that first game was another week at school and as the game got closer, the excitement mounted. My mate that I was going with followed Leeds United and had given me a lot of stick as Leeds United were such a massive team in those days and he knew, by coincidence that his team were the team that I used to follow!

On the morning of the match, we caught an early train from Dovercourt to Ipswich. It was in the days when there was considerably more standing room than seats in the ground and to stand a chance of getting in, you needed to be outside the ground queuing up by 11.30 in the morning at the latest, a far cry from today where guaranteed seats mean you can normally turn up as late as you like.

So by the time of the kick off, you had already been on your feet for at least four hours and nearly six hours by full time.

We didn't mind and time went quickly – there was an electric atmosphere and a real buzz outside the ground. We passed our time munching our packed lunches and talking to other supporters as well as watching the many Leeds United fans walking by.

Being a smallish lad of 11, whose previous live football experience had been being a regular supporter at Harwich and Parkeston's Royal Oak ground (still first result I look for after Ipswich), average crowd of about 150, the buzz and people watching really excited me and got the adrenalin going. I also remember thinking that the Leeds United supporters looked a bit intimidating and aggressive (or at the very least mouthy!).

The gates opened at about 12.30 and the long queue along the back of the Cobbold Stand (Portman Stand in those days) slowly edged forward. We took our place on the old Portman terrace towards the North Stand end of the ground.

Being our first match, we did not know anything about milk crates or boxes which smaller folk took to games in the days of terracing so that they stood a chance of seeing the game. We got a place behind a crush barrier halfway up the terracing which allowed us to see most of the pitch so we thought we would have a perfect view. We were well chuffed! However, it was only 12.55 by this time and still over two hours to kick off. As more and more people were jammed in it got tighter and tighter behind us and what was even worse, in front of us! I still have memories of police walking people alongside the pitch and putting people in to the terracing in front of us. It seemed very unfair.

No matter what, the atmosphere was unbelievable and I did manage one glimpse of the players walking the pitch but still with more than an hour to go. By 3.00, it seemed to me that all the biggest people in the ground were standing in front of me and my mate David. Of all the game, I can honestly say I saw less than 20 minutes action but could at least tell who was attacking by the roar of the crowd.

The full time whistle went and we were buzzing with excitement or maybe that's what is called adrenalin (do 11 year olds experience adrenalin?). The crowd, the songs, the atmosphere, – it would have been better if we had won, it would have been better if we had seen more than the backs of our fellow supporters but we'd know what to expect and what to do about it at the next game!

In those days, replays were played in the midweek immediately following the original match and I was still hopeful that the new team I was becoming a supporter of would beat the old team that I followed. Maybe it was blind optimism (based on seeing very little at the first game and not realising how intimidating Elland Road could be) but one could dream. The epic went on to not only that first replay at Elland Road but also two further replays played at Filbert Street in Leicester. Clive Woods took Town through with a wonder goal I still remember vividly. I was too young to attend but listened on the radio.

The next game at Portman Road was to get me hooked as a supporter forever. We got to the ground even earlier with our newly acquired milk crates and oh, what a match it was! It was Newcastle United at home and despite Ipswich winning, for some reason

Malcolm Macdonald stood out in my memory as he scored two or three goals that day and still ended up on the losing side. I also remember him scoring all five for England a couple of years later at Wembley against Cyprus, I believe.

Despite another big crowd, it wasn't of the Leeds United size which incidentally, still stands as the record crowd at Portman Road coinciding nicely with my first game. We stood in the opposite corner of the ground on the West Stand terrace (Co-Op nowadays), coincidentally, very close to where I still have my season ticket today, despite having spent seasons in all four stands during the years. We managed to get right to the front and had a fine view perched on top of our crates.

Town went in 3-2 down in an exhilarating first half, but little were we to imagine that it would get even better in the second half with a remarkable comeback and Ipswich ending up 5-4 winners at full time. The Geordies brought many supporters who brought their own songs and sense of humour that added to the atmosphere. They still are some of the most fanatical supporters I have ever seen. From that day on I have always had a bit of a soft spot for them too, only strengthened by the Ipswich connection of Messrs Robson, Dyer, Ambrose and Bramble.

Nine goals in my second match with a perfect view of all of them, Town the winners, that atmosphere again – it felt like a million miles instead of 20 from the Royal Oak and Harwich and Parkeston. I was becoming an Ipswich Town supporter and had started that adventure towards the 1000 games. Little did I dream at this stage that I would pass the 1000 mark against Norwich City (of all people) and appear on television, radio and in the paper to mark the occasion. I would also score a goal for Ipswich Town, and become the Ipswich Town Superfan on the way.

I didn't miss a home game for the remainder of the season seeing five games and five further wins.

David, my mate who attended the Leeds game with me, despite being a Leeds United fan had seen enough to be persuaded to join me in buying a season ticket in future years.

The journey had well and truly began despite hardly being able to claim love at first sight, more a case of lack of sight! There were certainly some remarkable stories to follow. Read on...

CHAPTER 2

THE REST OF THE '70S INCLUDING WEMBLEY '78

From that first game against Leeds United, I rarely have missed a home game to this day but in those early days, the only way I was going to get to an away game was through the kindness of my parents who didn't even really like football (no they weren't Norwich supporters – who is?) I was, however, soon doing paper rounds as soon as I was old enough and ended up working morning and evening to finance my growing hobby.

My first away game was, coincidentally, also against Leeds United in September 1975 and I was to see a number of matches at Elland Road over the years, mainly thanks to my family ties to that area of the country.

There were some special matches in the 70s. In 1975/76, I saw my first European match, a 2-0 home win over a good Fejenoord side in the UEFA Cup. Some great European nights followed in the 70s and the UEFA Cup is another story to be told (Chapter 6); who can ever forget the two wins over Barcelona in particular?

The 1976/77 season saw the home debut of probably one of my favourite, if not favourite players, Paul Mariner and what a welcome to Portman Road. It was a 7-0 hammering of WBA. Mariner was awesome and got a fantastic goal but was eclipsed by his partner up front, Trevor Whymark who scored four goals. There was also a certain Kevin Beattie who scored an unstoppable long range effort and I am sure if Osborne, the WBA keeper had got in the way, it would have taken him into the back of the net!

1977/78 was a season, I will never forget for several reasons – there was that 3-0 home win over Barcelona in the UEFA Cup (I choose to forget the second leg result!). It was a very mediocre League season but a fabulous Cup run in the FA Cup. The Semi Final at Highbury stood out as a very dramatic game and the immense feeling of relief and excitement at the final whistle knowing that we were finally going to appear at Wembley. I think realisation sank in as the third goal hit the back of the net but you could never be quite sure until that final whistle blew. Then we knew we had made it.

It was then that the nightmare started. Despite having attended all of the home games that year, due to a lack of funds that year, I was not a season ticket holder and a typical unorganised 14 year old. Announcements were made on ticket arrangements and I could not find my vouchers anywhere! I think to this day that I was so disillusioned with the league season that I never contemplated needing them! Tickets went quickly and reality soon set in that there was little or no chance of being part of Town's greatest day to date. But... Friday May 5th 1978 and there was a knock at the door and a magical moment in my footballing life was about to happen. Derek Parish, a neighbour in the Essex Police Force had some contacts and had not only obtained me a ticket but in the right end of the ground – the Tunnel End. I am eternally grateful – yet again thank you Derek.

The next issue was travel but I would have walked if I had to, however, fortunately, the Harwich branch was running a couple of buses and had a spare seat.

It was an amazing occasion from the minute I got onto the coach until the minute I got back – it felt like there was blue (Ipswich) and red (Arsenal) everywhere. I am not sure that they were all heading for Wembley or following it on the television but it did look that way! There was certainly a fair few Arsenal supporters setting off for Wembley even from as far away as Harwich and many Ipswich Fans.

It was in the days that alcohol was not banned from coaches so several folk were well merry by Colchester.

It was a fairly slow trip down to Wembley and I recall going through several villages and towns such as Manningtree and Colchester. The most memorable thing was the number of places decorated in Blue and White (ok well there was a bit of red and white as well but nowhere near as much!).

You could feel the excitement and tension building as you approached Wembley through the North London Suburbs. We joined the long queue of buses and coaches heading for the official car parks outside the Stadium and although we must have queued for at least an hour, we were still parked and off the coach by 12.30. One of my ambitions was to walk down Wembley Way as one of many Ipswich Town supporters (I had seen this happen for many years when BBC and ITV used to cover all day from about 10.00 in the morning but it had always been the supporters of somebody else – now it was my turn to do it following my team.) I left the coach behind and joined the many thousands mingling – they were a nice bunch on the coach but I did not know them so this was going to be my own experience shared with no one else. It was a magical experience approaching from the direction of the station and the thing that struck me as you looked down towards Wembley Stadium was the almost even divide of those in Red and those in Blue – quite a sight with the Twin Towers in the distance. Little was I to know that I would be looking at an almost identical sight from virtually the same spot 22 years later (v Barnsley Division 1 Play off Final, May 2000).

It was a fantastic atmosphere but I still remained a little cautious because Arsenal fans did have a bit of a reputation for their unpleasantness. However, it did appear that the occasion was getting the better of any potential trouble. Coincidentally, I did learn many years later that my wife's uncle had been hit by an Arsenal fan outside the turnstiles but I saw no bother.

I entered the ground well before 2.00 to soak up the atmosphere. It was unbelievable and I remembered even enjoying the things that were not normally my cup of tea such as the Band and Abide with Me.

We were in the tunnel end, I believe, thought to be the lucky end and I remember thinking we'd need every bit of luck we could muster as we were playing the mighty (so they thought!) Arsenal.

The match kicked off and simply flew by. I remember us hitting the woodwork twice, if not three times and being all over them but the ball would just not go in (sound familiar? Only today it's against teams like Walsall and Reading (no offence intended to them)).

The longer it went on, the more it felt like we might just never score but then that magical moment – a ball in, Willie Young, I believe stuck a leg out, out to Local Boy to become Instant Hero, Roger Osborne and it was at long last nestling in the back of the net. I still remember him becoming so overcome when all the team jumped on top of him that he had to go off and be replaced by Mick Lambert. But he had done his job. An all time hero at Ipswich.

Mick Mills went up to collect the FA Cup – it still seems like yesterday and will always be one of my great footballing memories.

Another memory that stood out was the journey home up the A12 (once we finally got out of the car park). I think every car and coach and bus was carrying Ipswich Town supporters – it was a long slow journey home but the sight of all the bridges over the A12 had to be seen. I reckon you could count on one hand the number of bridges over the A12 that weren't either decorated in blue and white with flags, scarves and banners or had people standing and waving and it was like that all the way home.

The team had a parade on an open top bus on the Monday, I believe, followed by a civic reception at the Town Hall. I was over to Ipswich in good time and walked with the bus for a long time, so long in fact that I got to the Town Centre behind 10s of thousands of fans that had gone straight there so I could not even get onto the square. I was dismayed but a quick thinking lad had seen a way up the scaffolding outside Debenhams and onto the roof so I followed – we had a fantastic view despite my fear of heights but more and more people joined us until it was quite unsafe. By then, the police had cause for concern and came up to persuade us to leave (you might think a difficult task but as the alternative was to spend time in a cell for trespassing, not too much effort was needed by an official chap in a different sort of blue!) I ended up not seeing any of the ceremony on the Town Hall Balcony but caught the highlights on the news later. I seem to recall I was not terribly honest with my mum about why I was home in such good time but as a 15 year old, was not too keen to mention my first brush with the law!

Well, I have spent the first two chapters reminiscing the early years of my love affair with Town now known as The Tractor Boys, from the next chapter onwards; the real action and adventures begin.

CHAPTER 3

THE COCKNEY BLUES, TRAINS AND TRAINERS

This chapter will probably bring back the memories of those long time supporters who followed their teams all over the country in the late seventies and early eighties.

Who can ever forget the casually dressed, difficult to identify supporter (I think in Ipswich Supporters cases it was safer on the trains when travelling in relatively small numbers) but for the other clubs supporters we ran across, it was so they could not get picked out by police or other clubs supporters until they were ready for whatever (and we certainly witnessed lots of whatever over the years!). The standard dress issue appeared to be the trainer shoes (normally Adidas), skin tight jeans or often, cords and some frighteningly loud jumpers you would not be seen dead in nowadays! There would often also be the pin button badge of the club that an individual followed. This could be quickly removed or covered. For some reason, other London Club Supporters normally hated us; I don't know whether it was because we were a supporters club full of mainly Londoners supporting a club from out of the City or what. We knew why Millwall hated us after the trouble in the FA Cup at The Den in 1978, Arsenal had a bit of a reputation, Tottenham had some real trouble makers and as for Chelsea and West Ham, watch your backs at all times.

I travelled to many away games in the late 70's and early 80's as this was the cheapest and most economical way to travel. I bought an under 24's rail card which entitled half price rail travel and this did save me a lot of money. I then discovered that it would be cheaper to join the Cockney Blues thus buying a half price ticket to Liverpool Street and then having a vastly subsidised ticket through the London Supporters Club to our destination from whichever London Station. In those days, they normally had one coach on a certain train departing from London reserved for us and the same on the way back from wherever we had been. However, as we approached the Bobby Ferguson era in the early eighties, away support by this method was dwindling and there was not that many travelling this way by the time I found cheaper and more convenient alternatives.

Later in this chapter, I will share with you my top six most memorable away games by train but firstly, I would like to remember some of the characters that I met during this era.

The first is Chris, I am still mates with him and he is a successful businessman who still lives down in Kent. We went to all the away games together and had some great times. Chris could sell sand to the Arabs; he had a gift of talking himself in and out of trouble. I always remember one of his scams when we were real young and destitute lads was to get us in to home and even a few away games free. I do now feel guilty about this but at the time, we just viewed it that if we saved the money, it would mean more away games we could attend to support our beloved team. Now his dad was a press photographer and had a pass but in those days, there was no photograph on it. We would meet up outside and show this pass at the entrance to the ground (let's take Portman Road for instance), outside the old ticket office. The steward would then let us in to the old Churchmans stand and we would walk straight through the back to the little side gate on the far side (Portman Road), Chris would wave his pass and make a point of having a long chat with the steward and then say that we were just going to the Centre Spot for a drink, but make sure he remembered us and could he let us back through? By this time, him and the steward were friends and we got back in to watch the match free later on. The record number he got in to the ground was four people. I often wondered why none of the stewards queried that the rest of us did not have a pass but they weren't always the brightest in those days. Thanks Chris and sorry to the club for doing this but it probably meant we made an extra 5-6 away trips so it was in a good cause. I lost touch with Chris when I stopped travelling by train but coincidentally we got married (not to each other) on the same day in 1988 and he saw a message in the Town programme so got back in touch with me and we have stayed in touch and attended games ever since.

The next character was big Nigel, a lad six foot plus tall and also probably across – he looked like a right ruffian but had a heart of gold and was always there for you. We travelled together to many games, the highlight being the UEFA Cup Quarter Final away to St Etienne, which we travelled all the way to the South of France by train (see Chapter 6). He was in the RAF for a long time and served in the Falklands. He always had a habit of saying the wrong thing at the wrong time (even in recent years, I remember being in a pub away to Crystal Palace when he said Palace were not very good in stronger terms – we were the only Town fans and I am sure would have got thumped if it was not for his two Palace mates we were with. He then rang them up in the middle of the game in the Palace end to tell them again and had to be asked to quieten down by one of the old bill!). That's Nigel for you. I am still in contact with him and see him at a home or away game occasionally for a pint. He lives in Sussex and works at Heathrow, moving planes around and even moved the plane that the Town Players were flying out to Sartid on when he worked at Gatwick.

Steve was a great mate to have but no one ever frightened him and if he got cornered or provoked he would usually hit first and ask later. His proven or unproven method was used at a Villa away game that was to result in me ending up with a fractured cheek bone (see chapter 8). He was in the RAF also I believe and later worked at Waitrose at Brent Cross and lived in North London. I, unfortunately, lost contact with him, although, I did run across him standing on the terraces at an away game at Watford several years ago. He was fairly worse for wear so I did not get contact details. Hope you are still alright and following the Tractor Boys Steve, maybe you are even reading this (I hope you agree with my description).

The last lad that I travelled regularly with was a lad called Podgy, he hailed from Chelmsford and was a bit of a nightmare – he always wore the same jeans and Black Leather Jacket that was too big for him (quite an achievement in itself hence the nickname!). He never actually travelled specifically with you and we never made any arrangements but he would always be there and end up with us usually scrounging drink or food. This was not surprising bearing in mind reservations out and back to London but bearing in mind the number of times that he would just happen to be on the same train out of many down to Liverpool Street, it was quite eerie! He would also normally end up in the same pub at an away venue or even in the same taxi or bus going to the ground. He could be a bit of a pain but was probably the loyalist of all of us as far as never missing a game. Are you still following them Podgy?

Ironically, whilst most of my adventures were with the Cockney Blues, the first one I remember happened on one of the old Blue Arrow Football Special Trains from Ipswich. It was Preston North End away in January 1980 in the FA Cup.

We travelled over to Ipswich in good time to pick up the Football Special that was to depart from Ipswich Railway Station. It was to be a five hour plus journey on one of British Rail's (as they were known in those days) more grubby specimens of a train (well, who in their right mind would have hired out a nice new train to football supporters in those days?). It went cross-country via Peterborough and as we went through the Midlands and on towards Manchester and the North West, it felt like a never-ending journey. Little was I to know that the journey back was going to feel even longer!

We arrived at Preston Railway Station about one o'clock where there were a large number of police waiting to meet us – it seemed a bit of overkill but they were to escort us to Deepdale, Preston's ground. It was a long and slow walk as there were probably about 700 – 800 of us. It was a typical Northern Town and there were a few Preston fans hurling their views and abuse from a distance and as normal the police kept a beady eye on any response from the away fans but were quite happy to turn a blind eye to the instigators.

Deepdale was not a touch on the ground it is today and I seem to recall even standing on a wooden terrace that bounced up and down as we sang and jumped about. The match was pretty uneventful with the Tractor Boys (as they are known nowadays) strolling to an easy 3-0 win. I did notice during the game a hard core of home supporters that were particularly vociferous and threatening but thought no more of it late in the game as they appeared to have had enough and dispersed with their side 3-0 down and going out of the cup.

We were kept in the ground for about 10 minutes and then the police spilt up the away supporters into those that had the short walk back to the coaches and the rest of us that had the long walk back to the railway station. As for those who came by car, that was their own problem (it is normal police policy to not care one little bit for these supporters as we would find out over the years).

As it was January, it was dark by full time so the walk back had an unappetising feeling about it, particularly as we entered a large park that we had to walk across. It was not terribly well lit as we walked down the main path through the park. To the left of us were a mixture of small trees, bushes and undergrowth and as we got further into this park you were aware of noises coming from the undergrowth to our left and shadows moving. All of a sudden, and over as quick as it had started a couple of Preston Fans ran across the 10-15 yards from the undergrowth to where the Town fans were walking, kicked, punched and head butted Town supporters and ran back into the undergrowth. We shouted at the police what was going on but as they could not see anything, they were not interested. This happened several times resulting in a total lack of response by the police who, understandably, had little interest in going into the undergrowth and getting set upon. It was a very clever ploy by these Preston fans as they were unlikely to get caught, we did not know how many there were and we also did not know if there was going to be a full on attack. I was not hit myself but I was pretty close and I was certainly glad to get out onto the road and leave the park behind us.

We got onto the train and with a good result behind us, but after the incidents in the park, we would certainly be glad to leave Preston behind us.

The train pulled out at about quarter to six and we were just settling down as the train gathered speed when bang, bang, bang and the train ground to a halt. We looked towards the window next to the table and seats that we were sitting in and there was a gaping, shattered hole where the window had been. I looked around and a chap opposite was throwing a brick back out of the window in the direction it had come from. There were several more thuds as bricks rained off the roof of our carriage and then there were sirens and blue lights as the police arrived (better late than never I suppose!).

I looked back around at the people sitting at my table and they were all looking at my right arm so I looked as well and it was covered in blood. I had not felt a thing. I had been putting my coat onto the over window rack and a brick (well half a brick actually) had gone through the window and landed where I had been sitting on the seat. My arm had taken the full blast of the shattered window but it could have been a lot worse if I had been sitting down at the time.

The train stopped for about 10 minutes, the Lancashire Police and British Rail Transport Police made a token walk up and down the train (I heard them saying that 8 windows had gone). They asked me if I wanted to go to hospital but there was no way I was going to spend any more time in that awful town than I could help and I would then have had the problem of getting home after.

The train started moving again and the guard on the train came down and cleaned me up and removed five or six shards of glass with tweezers as the train slowly made its way back South.

Unfortunately, as the train was full, there were no other seats so we had to put up with a bitter wind coming through the window as we travelled South so the coat was soon back on. In the end we all ended up sitting on the table opposite, as the bitter cold of a January night was just too much. I have never been back to Preston for football or anything since and have no intention to either!

My next memory of the train days was an away game at Everton in February 1980. Now, you might recall, but I am sure you will try to forget, Justin Fashanu's goal of the season against Liverpool when our beloved local rivals from Norfolk beat Liverpool 5-3 but I still swear to this day that I and 40 other hardy Town supporters witnessed a better goal scored by Eric Gates that day. It was just a shame that there were so few Town fans and so little TV coverage to back my views.

It was just like any other away game with the Cockney Blues, a train down to Liverpool Street and then a subsidised journey from Euston north to Liverpool Lime Street. We then got a taxi across Liverpool and the plan was to get a bus back, which was normally fairly safe as long as you kept quiet and didn't let on that you were not a scouser!

However, this time, the plan was not going to be quite so simple as Town wiped the floor with Everton winning 4-0 including that terrific strike by Eric Gates. I think because there were so few of us and even less going back by train, the Merseyside Police started to have serious concerns about our safety off the back of such a result.

Near the end, a Police Sergeant came over and said that we would be kept in for about 15 – 20 minutes to let some of the home fans disperse but then they would take the fans travelling by train back to Lime Street by Black Maria (Police transit van) for our own safety. There were 9 of us in the back of this van and it went at quite a speed so we bounced all over the place and I wondered whether this resulted in more bruises than if I was hit by a scouser?!

We got back to Lime Street much sooner than we would have done but the Police were still not happy as we still had 30 minutes to wait for the London train so they escorted us into a cafeteria on the station and stood at the door watching who came in. We all sat at the back of the cafeteria on three tables when a scouser we had seen at the ground started walking to the table with a Stanley knife (don't ask how he got past the police) but luckily they were still there and ran across the café and jumped on him before he had even got the cover off. By now, the train was in and the police escorted us to it but we were still a bit concerned in case any other trouble makers got onto the train and came after us but no-one was going to get past the barrier without a ticket so your average scouse trouble maker was not going to have the money to do that. There would be Everton supporters on the train but members of the London branch mainly who were just in the main loyal supporters, not trouble makers. However, we need not have worried, as there were four British Rail Transport police posted to our carriage just in case. The journey home was pretty uneventful after the rest of the day's close escape.

Moving onto the third of my top six memorable away games by train, I would name the Shrewsbury away game in the FA Cup in January 1981. This was the first game of several games we played up at Shrewsbury in the FA Cup in the eighties. They were well known giant killers and we managed one draw and two defeats in the three games. This game in 1981 ended up as a 0-0 draw and was the season when we won the UEFA Cup, made the FA Cup Semi Finals and were runners up in the league yet we still struggled to beat Shrewsbury over two games who were in the bottom depths of the Football League!

We left Euston on a large train and got off at Wolverhampton where we had to wait for half an hour to pick up a small local train out to Shrewsbury. There were no trains that went directly from London to Shrewsbury.

Anyway, we stood on the platform for about 10 minutes and then the announcer stated that the Euston to Holyhead boat train was due in a couple of minutes. We thought no more of it until it approached and these fearsome looking blokes were all head out of the window shouting about being the famous Millwall and no-one liked them (I could certainly see why people did take an immediate dislike to them!) (They had an away league match at Wrexham). The train drew to a halt and there was a spell of almost eerie silence (I think it was as the Millwall followers realised that there was a load of Ipswich Supporters on the platform). Now they have hated us probably more than most other team's fans since the Cup Slaughter (both on and off the pitch) in the FA Cup Quarter Finals at the Den in 1978 (Town won 6-1 and the game was held up for about 25 minutes due to fighting that day). I wondered what was going to happen but was already, instinctively edging towards the back of the platform when this lad down the platform in a broad Suffolk accent started singing "We went to Millwall --- we beat them 6-1". That was like a red rag to a bull or chucking a match in the firework box and all hell let loose as I was to witness my first ever Millwall Brick. This was a newspaper rolled tightly up and folded over twice and when someone is hit by it they know about it. There was also a massive Londoner with a baseball or rounders bat running down the platform so I had seen enough. I was next to the door to the ladies toilets so being not proud, I thought that this appeared to be a safe sanctuary so ran in, praying that there was a cubicle free – luckily there was. I ran in and locked the door and climbed onto the toilet seat in case anyone came in looking and waited for what seemed like ages (probably a maximum of 2-3 minutes but it felt like forever).

I then heard the announcement that the Holyhead train was departing so I left it another couple of minutes until I heard it pulling away and then cautiously stuck my head out of the door. All was quiet – there were a few people nursing themselves where they had been punched and kicked but apparently there had been only a small number, albeit violent, of about 25 Millwall followers who had ran the length of the platform and jumped back on at the other end of the train (it had sounded as though there were hundreds but whereas there may often be hundreds of supporters milling around trouble, only a few actually get involved, every one of the Millwall was today which made them an awful enemy). I had expected to see loads of police trying to sort it out but I expect as it was over as quick as it started and there were only a couple of British Rail Transport Policemen at the station, they preferred to let the boat train go on its way and be someone else's problem, elsewhere.

After all this drama, the game was a pretty uneventful 0-0 draw spoilt by a poor view and jam packed into a tiny stand that had far too many fans squashed into it (in those days, the UEFA Cup winning year, everybody wanted to see Ipswich play).

We could not leave the ground quick enough, with one thing in mind, to get the earliest local train back to Wolverhampton and make sure we were ahead of the Millwall followers returning from Wrexham. We got a train shortly after five and were back at Wolverhampton in plenty of time. We looked at the large timetable and the first train from Wrexham after their game had finished was at least half an hour away. Our train arrived on time (it would be typical if British rail were late but they weren't) and we were back at Euston ahead of the Millwall followers that did not like us. I never did see the lad that sang back at Millwall again all day so I don't know whether they got him or he'd been so scared he had gone straight home!

Another memorable away game by train, 4th on my list was the away game at Coventry, again in the UEFA Cup winning year in February 1981, which Ipswich won 4-0. This result came as a great tonic to the previous year we'd played there and lost 4-1. I have since seen Ipswich score four a couple of other times at Highfield Road in 4-2 wins including last season (2002/03) after being 2-0 down.

Games stand out in my mind when specific incidents happen and this one was not short of a few incidents. It all started with a late morning arrival at Coventry railway station from Euston. We had a lot of time on our hands so when faced with a look around the shops or a pint or two in the pub, what would you do? Yes we headed for a pub! We found a large non seedy looking establishment and went in to the lounge bar trying to look inconspicuous but five or six non locals with no Midland twang to their accent were pretty obviously away supporters to the locals despite having no colours on. However, we got talking to several of the Coventry supporters and they did not seem a bad bunch. Little did we know they were setting us up for later. Stupidly, we were so at ease with the surroundings, we let our guard down and stayed there until about quarter past two. In the meantime, all the locals we had spoken to had gone apart from two or three of them.

We started making our way the half mile or so to the away end at Highfield Road and noticed that these two or three were following us about 300 – 400 yards behind us but were not doing anything to raise suspicions so far. We turned down this side street off the main road towards the ground and all of a sudden there was a roar and about 20 or 30 Coventry fans, nearly all of them that I recognised had been at that pub, came from two directions. We were odds on for a hiding – did we run down the middle of the road and dodge the cars as well as these louts intent on giving us a hiding or take the pavement route? Luckily, I spotted Steve opting for the pavement route and his path was only blocked by one Coventry fan that did not look that confident facing up to Steve (not many people would do) so Steve just ran straight at him head down and his head must have caught him between stomach and chest. This not only had the result of winding him but putting him straight over a small wall and ornamental hedge into someone's front garden. I needed no second invitation seeing my escape route and don't think I had ever run so fast in my life. I was at the away end before I knew it and quite happy to pay my money and get into the sanctuary of the visitor's end. I had noticed police running the other way and that had saved the other's who had opted for the road route from getting too much of a hiding. Not a nice place!

We thoroughly enjoyed the game and saw a resounding 4-0 win, Alan Brazil at his best and I seem to recall a terrific goal from Steve McCall.

We made a very low profile walk back to the station and managed to avoid our so-called friends from the pub the previous lunchtime.

We got the Inter City back to Euston and about half way through the journey, a very excited Podgy came back to announce that Jimmy Hill was sitting in the First Class carriage, two coaches down. Now Jimmy Hill was not only a director or something at Coventry but also that well known TV Pundit on Match of the Day that had great delight in bad mouthing Ipswich. So bearing in mind his involvement at Highfield Road both in a club and television capacity (Town were on Match of the Day that night), we felt it would be interesting to have a chat! About 20 of us made an impromptu visit to First Class to ask Jimmy what he thought of the way Ipswich dismantled his team and also asked him how he intended to slag Ipswich off on Match of the Day that evening after that result. He was quite keen to praise Ipswich and tell us how he had always admired them but not that we would have laid a finger on him (however tempting!). I got the impression he felt intimidated and thought that was the most sensible thing to say! I did not believe him. Anyway, we arrived at Euston and had great pleasure in following him down the platform singing about the size of his chin. Not surprisingly, he did not seem that amused and was no doubt glad to see the back of us (a mutual feeling!). He was reasonably complimentary for a change that night on Match of The Day so we'd like to think it was our good influence!

Just to bring this away day to Coventry to an end, there was just time for a swift pint in Dirty Dicks just outside Liverpool Street, however, there was a load of Everton fans who quickly started lobbing beer glasses and turned the bar into an all out brawl. We left in a hurry thinking we'd had enough for one day but I do hate leaving almost a whole pint!

Fifth in the list was Swindon away, in a pre-season game and I cannot recall if it was a friendly or a testimonial for one of the home team, I believe the latter. This was an absolute nightmare from start to finish but thankfully not due to unruly opposition fans but down to awful transport. I was working in Colchester at the time and left at four to get a train down to London – looking at the timetables, there was plenty of time with two choices of train to get out of Paddington to Swindon. Unfortunately, I had not reckoned on points problems and the overhead cable problems. It took double the time to get to Liverpool Street and I arrived at Liverpool Street by about twenty past six giving me precisely five minutes to get across London to get the later of the two trains I had noted were my options. Did I give up there and then – not on your life, I jumped in a black cab and headed for Paddington and got there about five to seven. By the time I got a train out of Paddington, it was not scheduled to get there until 25 minutes after the kick off but at least this train was on time. I got into Swindon and jumped in another cab and got to the ground half an hour after kick off. I then could not find a way into the ground (as most of the turnstiles had shut) for another 5-10 minutes and finally found a turnstile that gave me access to the main stand five minutes before half time. The game, does not stand out at all, I was knackered!

I then got the trains home, all on time but unfortunately, the train out of Liverpool Street around about eleven thirty was too tempting and I fell sound asleep. As this was the most popular train back to

East Anglia after a Friday Night out in London, a lot of people had similar ideas so I was nothing out of the ordinary. I awoke to a much quieter train and discovered, I had slept through a number of stations including Manningtree where I was to get off and was well on my way to Norwich of all places! I was then stuck there until the first train out at about 0500 in the morning so did not get home to Dovercourt until 0700 the next morning. All for 50 minutes of pre-season football!

My last memorable train journey was for all the wrong reasons, DRINK! I do still however still blame my so-called mates for it. We were faced with an extremely long train journey down to Wales from Paddington for the away game at Swansea so they decided to find something to do to while away the time! They decided to play a form of Russian roulette but using cards and spirits. We played all sorts of games such as Pontoon and the loser of each hand had another short tipped into the British Rail plastic cup. Now I am an awful card player, Snap being my limit so my beaker was soon pretty full and by the time I had drunk this concoction, particularly being a non-spirit drinker as well, I was very much the worse for wear. I was not sick on the way to the ground but I remember feeling awful when the fresh air hit me and I do not remember getting from the station to the ground. Maybe my mates looked after me, feeling guilty after getting me into this state?! Anyway, I saw no more than 10 minutes of the game and was either being ill in the loos or sitting on the steps at the back of the stand.

The journey home was awful, and I sat in First Class, as the train was half empty. I remember Frank McClintock, the ex Arsenal player looking at me as I got up to try and get to the loo and asking if I was OK as I looked a bit pale just as I was sick again. I still to this day do not know if I actually managed to pebble dash his immaculate jacket or not so if I did Frank, I am really sorry and can assure you that it was nothing personal (now if that had been Jimmy Hill that could well have been a different matter!).

Graeme Brooke

CHAPTER 4

ON THE BUSES (WELL COACHES AND MINBUSES)

Away games on coaches was a natural progression from going away by train and this method tended to coincide with a drop in numbers including my mates who were travelling away by train. Of my mates in the Cockney Blues, Nigel was to move around with the RAF and Steve and Chris just gradually lost their enthusiasm. That really left the inimitable Podgy who you would not really wish to be your only specific travelling companion.

So I then discovered away travel by coach on a more regular basis. I had travelled to the FA Cup Final in 1978 with the Harwich branch but I was now using the Club Supporters coaches that went from Portman Road and more often, the supporter's coach from Clacton. As I gained more experience behind a wheel, hiring a minibus then became the more regular way to travel.

My first real memory of coach travel other than that FA Cup Final trip was another day out at Shrewsbury. It was the second of two defeats we experienced and was memorable for all the wrong reasons. There was the defeat; there was a fight in the away end against a large group of Telford United supporters (don't ask me why?) Apparently, they had been due to play a big game that had been called off so being as Telford is only a short drive away, they decided to come down and cause trouble. I don't know how they got tickets as I thought it was all ticket? Anyway, I have never been but understand that Telford is one of these really rough modern overspill towns where a lot of the residents appear to have nothing better than to pick fights all day! I remember hearing in the ground long after the Telford fans had been kicked out that plans were afoot by some Town fans to head to Telford for revenge after the match. I remember sitting on the Club coach going down the motorway or dual carriageway and seeing three minibuses parked on the hard shoulder on the slip road into Telford but never did hear whether they did venture into Telford to gain retribution or whether they were parked there as a symbolic gesture as all the coach convoy went past. No one really cared as we were out of the Cup for the second time to these awful giant killers. I vowed never to go back and have not been back since.

The coaches made steady progress and were scheduled to stop for a comfort stop at the Watford Gap service area on the M1. We were all aware that Norwich City, our hated rivals had played at West Bromwich Albion also in the FA Cup but thought no more of it. In those days, football supporters coaches had to book into a motorway service area in advance so there would be no issue as there was no way that they would allow Ipswich and Norwich coaches to be at the same service area, let alone at the same time. How wrong could we be?

When we arrived, there were loads of coaches but that was a common occurrence. We got off the coach and walked across the Car Park and up the steps into the main foyer. There was loads of yellow and green of Norwich and of course having been the victims of a giant killing, we were going to be on the receiving end of some serious stick from our canary coloured rivals.

We walked into the self-service restaurant and did our best to ignore the ribbing as the budgies (slang amongst Town supporters for Canaries) supporters were due to leave any minute. However, this was the budgie's heaven, their main rivals down after a giant killing and a chance to gloat – they were in no hurry to leave despite being summoned to their coaches. Then it all started, some drinks and some food were thrown and then cutlery and plates started getting hurled. There was fighting starting all around the service area. The worst of it was across the car park but luckily police arrived within a minute or two, so I don't know if they had been called in advance by someone who anticipated that the worst was about to happen. The scenes were disgraceful despite the fact that the police turned up in a short space of time and there was no excuse for it, no matter how much you dislike your local rivals. However, the service area had to shoulder some of the blame for accepting Ipswich and Norwich coaches at the same place at the same time. Although, they rarely play away at the same time, I have never seen it be allowed to occur since.

I would guess the most memorable away trip by mini bus was the first one that I drove to which was up to Newcastle United for a League Cup (or Milk Cup – a cup that has had more names than Elizabeth Taylor!) replay in November 1984. We had drawn the first game down at Portman Road and if I remember rightly, had not performed well at all. From memory, there was one half full coach that went from Portman Road plus our minibus making a total away support of around the 40 mark. No one gave us much hope so next to no one fancied that trip all that way up north for an away game with little or no chance of winning on a midweek evening.

We picked the minibus up from the hire company in Colchester and drove to Grantham Service Area on the A1 where we filled up with fuel. The plan was then to drive up the A1 to Washington Service Area where we were to meet up with the other coach and the police escort. We did this and were escorted to a prime parking position on the hard standing behind the away end. This looked as safe as we could ask for.

We went into the ground and even for a League Cup replay with the away team bringing next to no supporters (or so we thought!), the atmosphere was buzzing. We looked around and as we approached kick off, the away end was very well populated – it was filling up with Newcastle supporters. We were considerably outnumbered! Luckily Newcastle scored earlyish and they all jumped up and the police were up to the task, marching them all out. That was more like it – around about 40 of us on a terrace for a few thousand. The team turned it around and won 2-1 against most people's expectations. I often wonder what makes me travel all that way to an away game when realistically, I have no expectation of a victory. It must be because results like this can always prove you wrong.

Obviously winning at St James's Park is never best for the away supporters health and the home team fans were not happy. The police kept us in for about 20 minutes to let them clear. The police then laid on a high-speed escort out of Newcastle and onto the A1. They had first spoken to the drivers (that was me on the minibus and the supporters club coach driver) and said that they would escort us 10 miles down the A1 and then we would be on our own and on no account to stop until we were a long way from Tyneside! We travelled at speeds of up to 60 mph with loads of police bike riders blocking all roads so we could go straight through any red lights and roundabouts. It was just as well as a load of Geordies ran down one side street and were hurling anything they could lay their hands but there were no bangs on the mini bus so they missed!

We left the police escort and were aware of a car with its headlights on full beam following us for ages. In the end I slowed down and it did go past us – it was a little Fiesta with five large Geordies that were shoehorned in to it but the one in the front still managed to do a moony to us as they went past whilst his mates hurled abuse. They then slowed down forcing us to go past and this went on for miles but there was no way we were going to stop. We lost them somewhere near Doncaster thankfully as the next chapter of this trip was about to unfold.

Having filled up at Washington, the plan was to fill up again at Grantham to get us back to Colchester but little had we reckoned on the extra miles from Washington to St James's Park and back would be enough to make us run out of petrol about three miles short of Grantham. By this time, it was thick fog as well so not a good time or place to run out of fuel. Two of us set off and managed to hitch a lift quite easily with a lorry driver who stopped cause he saw the hazard warning lights. The others slept or dozed or drank the remains of the beer!

We got to Grantham and found a large can on some roadworks nearby so filled it up. The next issue was hitching a lift – who in their right mind would pick two blokes up at 3am in the morning with a dodgy can full of petrol. In the end we decided to walk back onto the forecourt and of the first couple of people we asked, one was heading south and the other locked all his doors. My mate decided drastic action was needed and stood in front of this Transit Van filling up and was not going to move but there was no need for such action as I spoke to the driver who was happy to help. By this time the fog had come down thicker and it was really difficult to even see the hazard warning lights but we got back and were on our way again. After a quick refuel and a coffee at Grantham, we got back to Colchester after dropping everyone off and me calling round to Dovercourt to put my suit on for work at ten to eight, ten minutes before I would have had another half days hire to pay for! I then went straight to work and felt pretty rough for the next couple of days. The things we do for a game of football!

Another brief memory was an away game at Coventry City in November 1984, three days after our long night at Newcastle (see previous story) to be precise. It was a thoroughly disappointing defeat and we were sitting in traffic waiting for traffic lights to change when a couple of Coventry fans started giving it some over the road – Now after the defeat, (it was not the defeat itself but the manner that the Town looked like they'd just given up and died), we were not happy bunnies on the minibus and someone decided to open the backdoors and tell these two Coventry fans exactly what they thought of them (do you get the drift?!) With this whilst this lad was still on the back step, about 50 Coventry fans came hurtling across this park towards us. Our driver realised evasive action was needed and pulled out of the traffic and started to accelerate down the wrong side of the traffic with one of our travellers having been dislodged off the step running as quick as he could after it, with the Coventry followers coming after him about 100 yards behind! The minibus paused at the lights, which were still red, which enabled the occupants on the minibus to put hands out, and grab him just as the lights changed. We accelerated away with the back door still swinging and our colleague head first over the back seat and feet still sticking out much to the Coventry gangs amusement, who had, by this time given up the chase. We certainly had a few close shaves at Coventry, it's just not a pleasant place – it does not seem to matter whether you win or lose or whether it is before or after a game, they are always looking for a scrap. The safest way to go there appears to be one or two of you in a car with no colours but even then, you need to be very careful what area you park in!

My fourth memory of the minibus days was overshadowed by tragedy at another ground 150 miles away. It was May 11th 1985, the day of that terrible fire at Valley Parade, Bradford when 56 Football Supporters perished. It was Ipswich's last away game at Sunderland and as tradition has it, the Ipswich fans enjoyed attending this end of season bash, the last away game in fancy dress. We had hired a 15 seater minibus from Colchester that was packed with 15 Town supporters varying from School Girls to Bugs Bunny, Pink Panther and at least a couple of Gorillas. I was the driver and dressed especially for the occasion as a Gorilla, complete with mask (some would still say that I did not need it and looked scarier without it! Of course, I would have to disagree!)

We had the normal call in at Grantham Services where it was quite busy with supporters off coaches all (at least 90% in fancy dress). We filled up with fuel but were not going to make the same mistake, as the Newcastle game and drove to Scotch Corner where we were going to fill up again and have a swift pint in the Hotel. I cannot recollect why we chose to have a drink there but only a few actually got a drink as we were accosted by a group of pensioners from the USA on a coach tour. They thought it was so quaint that a group of English Supporters were dressed up as Bugs Bunny, Pink Panther, and Gorillas etc they just had to have photos to take home. We must have posed for all 50 of them and it felt like ages. It would have been an advantage to have been wearing something a lot plainer so I could have got to the bar but I don't suppose I would have been drinking anything much more exciting than a Coke as I was the designated driver anyway! The Americans were telling us that all they ever heard of about Soccer in the USA was the trouble and hooliganism and I think we were a real eye opener for them. It must be said that this is quite often the case with Town fans when they travel home or abroad, how they gain good commendations for their good behaviour and humour.

We left our new found American Friends who were heading off for Edinburgh and headed onto the game at Sunderland. We arrived in good time at about two o'clock just after the coaches or so we thought. As for the 14 passengers, they were in plenty of time but that was not so for the driver, yours truly! The police plan was to drop the supporters off outside the away end and then escort the coaches and minibuses to a deserted coach park about four or five miles away on the coast. We got there at five to three parked and then the debate started, as there were three minibus drivers including myself and originally the police had planned to leave the drivers with their vehicles until they escorted them back to collect the passengers at full time. We went ballistic at the officer in charge and in the end, at ten past three they laid on a police minibus to take us and two or three of the official coach drivers back. It must have been quite a sight seeing a five foot 10 inch gorilla arguing with a Makem police officer but the gorilla had a partial victory. I say partial as we did not get back to Roker Park until twenty five past three (police officer driving so could not break the speed limit could he!)

Sunderland away at the old Roker Park

I joined up with my group and it felt like I had only just settled down to watch the game when a loudspeaker announcement asked for all Coach and Minibus drivers to meet outside the Away section at four thirty to be driven back to the coach park. I was fuming and was sure that it had been that awkward Makem officer in charge that had arranged it. I did argue the point on the police minibus and pointed out that I would have driven a minibus on and off for best part of 15 hours to see only 50 minutes out of 90 minutes football. One of the other minibus drivers was a full time driver and not too worried as he was being paid but the other one was a supporter like me and was lucky not to be arrested for what he said on the way back to the coach park.

We made our way back to Roker Park in convoy and picked our passengers up and I think they did feel sorry for me as they said that it was not a good game and I had not missed much. That was not the point and I had missed 40 minutes in fact. It was one miserable monkey driving back down the A1.

As we travelled south, my miserable attitude and the boisterous alcohol enhanced spirit of the passengers evaporated very quickly to one of utter sadness as the events of Valley Parade where 56 supporters had died in that terrible fire unfolded over the radio. Although we stopped for a quick pint, it was only a quick pint as much to stretch our legs and it was a very subdued journey home to say the least.

Now the mid 80s were certainly the maddest years for minibus trips and no one came madder than Phil who ran a lot of these minibus trips. The things he would get up to were quite unbelievable and he always got away with it. One of his tricks was to have a box of eggs in the minibus and anyone that upset him or took the micky out of us would normally have an egg lobbed out the window and would be hit more often than not!

The Leicester away game in September 1985 springs to mind as a good example of Phil's craziness. We were doing the cross-country route over to Leicester from the A1 (in the days before the A14 was built from Huntingdon to the M1 and M6). We got stuck behind this coach load of Wisbech fans, a non-league Eastern Counties League side that happened to be rivals of Braintree at the time. By chance one of the lads on our minibus was from Braintree direction and had a Braintree Scarf. Now the lads on the back of the coach were fairly abusive towards us before they saw this scarf being held up but were plain offensive after and Phil was getting more and more jarred off. All of a sudden we arrived at a roundabout and we went off in a different direction to the Coach, Phil decided he was going to get past them by going the wrong way around it. Unfortunately for us, a couple of old dears in a Metro came the other way and we just missed them and did have to slow down so we did not get past the coach. More abuse followed in a two-way exchange.

We got to the next roundabout and wondered what was going to happen and all of a sudden, as it was pretty flat, Phil accelerated, straight onto the roundabout and we approached some small conifer saplings as we exited the roundabout literally and accelerated away – we were past them and left them with a vision of two of our back seat passengers doing moonies out of the back window!

We parked at Leicester to be greeted with a suspicious eye from a traffic police officer looking at our roof rails and when we looked up noticed about a 2-foot length of conifer. When you combined this look with the mud down the side of the minibus, I suppose it did look a bit suspicious. The officer walked over to Phil and asked him to explain. Quick as a flash, Phil explained that we came from country parts and that seemed to satisfy the officer which was quite amazing as this was many years before we became known as the Tractor Boys.

Another end of season away game was to Bradford City, three years after the fire in May 1988. We went via coach and I was dressed as a farmer and Sharon, my wife (or fiancée at the time) went as a clown. This was a massive game for Bradford in the old second division (First Division equivalent today). We had had a pretty poor season and could do nothing (apart from stopping Bradford go up to the top flight for the first time in their history). Of course we just had to spoil the day and won 3-2. Their supporters rioted and attacked the away section through the stands, across the pitch and even tried to get at us through the closed turnstiles. It was very scary stuff and the only funny memory (if you can have any of football violence) was the sight of a pantomime camel or horse (obviously Town supporters) being chased across the pitch by Bradford yobs. Although, it is always the minority that spoils it for the others, there was certainly now a different feeling to that we had had to Bradford and its supporters three years earlier on the way home from Sunderland.

Seventh on the list is the Leeds United away game in the FA Cup 3rd Round in January 1990. This game was a nightmare to organise as far as the minibus due to the ticket arrangements at Elland Road. Leeds had decided that they weren't going to provide any seats, Ipswich appealed to the FA and so it went on. In the end Leeds relented and provided a very low number of seats and foolishly, the occupants of our minibus bought some, whilst the majority of the Town Supporters stood in the opposite corner of the stadium. As so few seats had been provided, we were not in a proper away section and occupied the front couple of rows of a strange area in one corner of the stadium. You would say that it was arguably upper tier, but all that separated us from the tier below was a very low wall immediately in front of where we were sitting.

The game was a normal cup-tie with the home side throwing everything at us but very ineffective up front. Ipswich broke forward and scored the only goal of the match and this did not please the home fans one little bit.

At the final whistle, the stewards said we were not allowed out and would be kept in for about 20 minutes but almost immediately, there were Leeds fans making their way up to the back of the lower tier. As soon as the first one came over the wall, three of us ran up the steps and pushed the steward aside – it would be far safer taking our chance outside mingling with the home supporters.

We got to the outer exit from the stand we were in and Nick was going to turn right to walk back to where the coaches and our minibus were parked. Now I know Leeds like the back of my hand (around the ground) so I grabbed him and Graham and we went in the opposite direction. We were going to go back the long way around because although we had no colours on, if we had turned right out of the ground, it would have been obvious who we were. It took us about five minutes longer but we saw several people back at the parking area that had either been hit or threatened and Nick acknowledged that it had been a wise move going the long way so that we were at least walking in the same direction as the majority of the Leeds fans.

We were part of a sizeable police convoy away from Leeds and onto the M62, which we left behind to join the M1 and head south. A quick comfort stop was had at Leicester Forest Services where we took great pleasure in taking the micky out of a carload of Leeds fans but then had to make a hasty departure as two coach loads of Leeds fans pulled in which would have left us heavily outnumbered.

We decided to have a celebratory drink and picked a country pub on the outskirts of Northampton just off the ring road heading for Bedford. It looked a friendly enough place but there were a large number of young lads in the public bar as we walked in and they appeared to be split into two groups. Within a couple of minutes of being served, although we were in the Lounge Bar, we could hear voices being raised and then fists started flying. Glasses started getting thrown as well. We had a problem as the only obvious exit was back out through the public bar. Luckily, one of our group had just come back from the loo and he said that there was a fire exit off the corridor to the loo. We quickly decided that it was time to leave before one or other or both gangs decided that it would be better entertainment attacking a minibus load of non-locals! After that, we simply headed for home, glad that we were all in one piece!

Following the Leeds United away game in the FA Cup, Town were drawn away to Barnsley in Round 4. Organisation of this one was much easier with plenty of people wanting to go on the minibus and tickets fairly readily available. It was ironical though, because, I had never been to Barnsley before the away league game in December and so little over a month later we were heading back there again (and it is a bit of a depressing place, hardly a holiday resort). When the draw came out, I remembered the last visit for one main thing – the ramshackle very tight old stand that we were sitting in and when I had to go to the loo during the game it felt like the stand all had to stand up and knew where you were going (may as well have been an announcement over the Tannoy!). However, when I got out there, it was bitterly cold and snowing and there was no roof over the loos. What was funnier was that someone was obviously doing "the number twos" and he shouted out in a broad Suffolk accent that he had never had a dump in the snow before. At least I was only doing the number ones!

Anyway, we had several ex colleagues on this minibus and the standing joke all day was that a lad called Peter could not get the hang of the sliding door to open or shut it. (He did in the end though – see next paragraph!)

I cannot remember the exact circumstances, but as I remember an OAP had left before the end of the game and had gone back to one of the coaches. He had then been threatened by some young lads who had stolen his wallet. As we left the ground, the police operation was getting into full swing and it was announced that occupants were going to be randomly searched as we left the Coach Park. This took a considerable length of time until the police gave up in the end. As if other Ipswich fans would attack one of their own? The police certainly weren't of the brightest in Barnsley.

At least by the time we got away, the traffic had died down. Well, we pulled away and were following a minibus from Bury St Edmunds and as we went around a corner these two lads about 15 or 16 years old stood across the road waving what looked like a wallet. Instantaneously, both minibuses did handbrake stops and a load of us jumped out. This was at the time that Peter finally (much to his horror!) got the hang of the door and it opened first time. two or three stayed to look after the minibuses but the rest of us went after these two lads assuming that this was the stolen wallet. I don't know what my wife, Sharon, thought at the time, as I left her sitting on the minibus. They soon had headed into a very dodgy area of flats and we quickly called off the chase. We thought it could be an ambush or their mates could have been doubling up behind to have a go at the mini buses. The rest of the journey home was pretty straightforward and uneventful. It was amusing as when we arrived back in Colchester, Peter had trouble with that sliding door again! He is the most non-aggressive character you could meet so I would guess that it was because he did not want to end the day out and get off the minibus as opposed to his keenness to chase Barnsley supporters earlier!

The last of my memories I am covering in this chapter was Newcastle United away, when we were first back in the Premiership. The date was 26th November 1994 and we travelled with the Clacton Supporters club. This was the first year back in the Premiership and it was in the days that Andy Cole was still a hero at Newcastle. We travelled up on the Clacton Supporters coach on the long journey up the A1 and the arrangement with the Tyneside Police was to stop at the Washington Service Area and await the police escort. We got there in good time at about twelve and were not due to be met until quarter past one. Not many were keen to sit in a motorway service area getting ripped off for over an hour and one of our number noticed a fairly large hole that had been smashed through a fence at the back of the parking area. It seemed like a good idea to see what was the other side so we had a look through and 50 yards down the road was an inviting looking pub. It seemed like a much better proposition to us so we spent an hour in there. The locals were friendly and said they quite often had visitors from away teams through the hole in the fence!

Later on we were met by the police and went in convoy to the ground. There was not a big away following that day and we had been given a small block of seats surrounded by Geordies!

I remember the noise inside the ground was deafening and Newcastle penned us in our own half for all of the match on the pitch. However, it looked like we would sneak a point that we did not deserve when in the 91st minute, Andy Cole fired Newcastle ahead and the Geordies were not singing but screaming at us "You're not singing any more". What a long way to come for nothing but we were wrong, two minutes later and in the last 30 seconds of injury time, Claus Thomsen won the ball and ran and ran from near the halfway line and banged in the equaliser. The roar turned to silence and disbelief as we celebrated. A chap with suicidal tendencies stood up as the noise died down and sang back "You're not singing any more" which as it rubbed the Geordies noses in it somewhat did not go down well at all!

We left the ground as soon as the whistle went but even then there were some Geordies milling around and I got punched as I walked away from the away end. We made our way back to the coach, parked at the opposite end to the away end. Great thinking by the police! I was glad to get onto the coach but was on the receiving end of lots of threats and abuse through the window until we pulled away. There were even police sitting close to the coach but they did not care. It seemed that they did not like anyone that was not from Newcastle and it was our fault that we supported a team that had stopped Newcastle winning!

I have travelled to many away games with the Clacton Supporters club on their coaches and although, only the Newcastle game (see last paragraph) is mentioned as a top memory, this is due to the fantastic work and effort Jill Lewis and Pat Edwards put into organising trips. They have enabled a lot of people to get to games that they would not, otherwise have got to, particularly night games. They run coaches at subsidised rates through fund raising and other activities and balance popular away trips against unpopular ones so prices are not too high. The organisation is always first class without a hitch and they provide a first class service for those supporters based across the border in Essex. The coach always has a nice bunch of people on it and I think because of the organisation and lack of a problem on a trip, that is why I do not have more memories. People like Pat and Jill often go unnoticed as they do such a good job and everyone takes them for granted, so I'd like to take this opportunity to say a big thank you.

The most memorable of all of my away trips by coach or minibus has got to be Wembley 2000 for the Play Off Final against Barnsley. That is a separate chapter in itself.

CHAPTER 5

CARS AND BARS

The main ingredients in the recipe for a good away trip by car were:

A full car load to keep the cost down

A win for the Tractor Boys

A nice pub with good food being cooked at lunchtime

No traffic jams on the way home

Now, those of you that have or still do attend away games by car will confirm that it is normally a very rare experience to achieve all of those ingredients and the recipe normally goes wrong. I don't think Delia Smith would achieve that too often if she swapped Budgies (Canaries) for Tractor Boys. That's why she should stick to her own type of recipes in the kitchen. Yes Delia, do something you're good at and fairly sure of success!

Travelling to away games by car was to become my most favoured form of transport, purely for convenience and cost. If you could get five in a car, it could cost half the price of an official coach trip and significantly less than a train trip (especially once too old for a young person's railcard!).

Another method I used to keep the cost down was to sponsor part of a players kit and this helped us get on talking terms with the players and they would normally get at least a couple of complimentary tickets and quite often, enough for the whole car. Two players I sponsored were Craig Forrest and Bryan Gayle. Johnny Wark was also good to me and often got me tickets. I attended 17 or 18 away games the season we got promoted from the old Second division to the inaugural Premiership and I only bought tickets for Leeds United away in the FA Cup, Southend away and the last match at Oxford. So for a sponsorship outlay of around £50, the free tickets for 15 or 16 games certainly made a massive net saving. The beauty then was that if you got five in a car and were not paying to get in, away games were often as cheap or cheaper than a home game and this meant we could afford a lot more away games than we would have done otherwise. Chris's scam with the press pass mentioned in Chapter 3 also was a good cost cutter!

My first highlight in the Car Journey era was an away trip for a pre season trip to Glasgow Rangers in August 1981. It involved a trip in my parent's car to Galashiels in the Scottish Borders and then a coach journey into Glasgow about 70 miles away. I was meeting my mum's friend's son who was a Rangers fan and was staying with them overnight. I was really excited, as Rangers were my Scottish team so it was a dream come true that Town were playing them.

We headed for Ibrox and as we approached the ground, I could not believe the numbers. Pre- season games that I had been to before were normally attended by a couple of thousand at most. Here, it was a sell out and there was upwards of 40000 people. Ipswich were a big attraction in those days, having won the UEFA Cup just two months earlier at the end of May.

It was a fantastic stadium even in those days, a mixture of modern and traditional. Ipswich played very well and won 2-1. It was an amazing feeling to see them win knowing that I was in the minority. I am sure I was not the only Town fan there but I did not see any others.

Second on the list of car journeys was another mad escapade to Scotland, nearly exactly a year later. It was Aberdeen away and as at ten on the Friday night before, I had no plans to go there but 10 hours later we were sitting eating breakfast in the service area near the Forth Bridge at Edinburgh well on our way to Aberdeen!

I was playing darts for the Royal London Social Club on Friday evening and got talking with one of my mates Martin about what we were doing for the rest of the weekend. The common theme was nothing! I said half jokingly, "you don't fancy an away trip to Aberdeen do you?" Amazingly, bearing in mind that Martin was a Chelsea and Colchester United supporter, he said yes why not. We hung around for the end of darts and got in contact with another of my mates who was actually a Town supporter and left Colchester at about eleven o'clock.

I don't think we had really quite appreciated how far it was – well on the map, it was straight up the East Coast and didn't look that far. In actual fact it was something like 600 miles. We had about an hour's snooze in a lay-by near Darlington but other than that, it was all the way to Edinburgh. I think adrenaline kept us going through the night. In 1982, cars certainly weren't as modern and comfortable as they are today and mine was no exception. It was a Hillman Avenger 1300 and I do not know how it or we survived the 1000 mile + round trip over three days!

My mother had a cousin in Aberdeen so by chance she had said in the past that I would be welcome to stay. She had a caravan in the front garden that they used to go away in so we headed there after the 1-0 victory in Drew Jarvie's testimonial. We did not know whether they'd be there but it was worth a try rather than driving straight back on the Saturday night. They were there and despite turning up without notice, they made us most welcome and we had a few beers at a motel just down the road from them. Davie had warned us not to go into the centre of Aberdeen in view of that afternoon's result!

We stayed for lunch and headed back south on Sunday afternoon arriving home about three on the Monday morning. I didn't see my parents until the next day and I think they were a bit disbelieving when they asked what I had got up to at the weekend as were some of my colleagues that had been in the darts team the previous Friday. I still do not think that they would have believed I had gone if it was not for the programme!

Number 3 on the list of car journeys was the away match at Old Trafford in May 1984. Some of you may remember that we had a pretty disastrous season that year and we were left needing points in our last two away games that just happened to be away to Liverpool at Anfield at the end of April and then away to Manchester United on 7th May 1984. We had done the business at Anfield, performing well and getting a creditable 2-2 draw but that left us really needing a win at Old Trafford and we got it. That was the good news but there was plenty of bad news beforehand!

There were five of us – four Town fans and your typical Manchester United fan, lived 200 miles away and rarely got to Old Trafford! (It was in the days prior to Sky subscriptions and he didn't wear the replica shirt that day as he was in the Town end so I'll leave those extra jibes out – only joking George!)

Now five in a mark 2 Escort 1300 on such a long journey was a squeeze and tiring at the best of times but this journey was one like no other! We got to just before Corley service area on the M6 near Coventry and the car started chugging and making funny noises. We could see no real signs of a problem when we stopped but none of us were mechanics!

We carried on and just before Knutsford services the car got even worse, if that was possible (it could only do 50mph maximum by then anyway!). By now it was twenty past two and getting close to kick off. We limped on and the one plus was that most of the traffic was already there and parked.

It was twenty past three by the time we got there and although tempting to give up, there was no way we would have, as it was such a crucial game. On entering the ground, it was buzzing and guess why? We were a goal down already! Our mate was pleased with the score but not happy that he had missed the goal (greedy or what!) Anyway Town went on and made a terrific comeback winning 2-1 and they were as good as safe. Our Manchester United mate was gutted – missed the goal and then saw them concede two and lose (now I know why they have so many fans that only watch them on the television – so at least they can switch them off when they are doing badly!). Things were going even worse for Shaky (our Escort owner). I had wondered where he had got to and he had apparently gone to the loo and some drunken or drugged up Manchester United supporter had been in there. Subsequently, he had tried to hit Shaky but fallen over. Shaky was then escorted from the ground by a copper that was not interested in either the truth nor what a Manchester United fan was doing in the visitor's section either! He was certainly in competition with George the Manchester United fan for biggest misery, you won George cause at least our team won – Shaky just missed some of it!

We headed south and what a journey – we pulled over on the hard shoulder, as the engine got worse and a Capri pulled up behind us – it was a chap called Kenny from somewhere down in Worcestershire and he was another Town fan. He said he'd follow us and help if he could – by now we were doing a maximum of 30 mph down the hard shoulder with the hazard warners on and Kenny following us doing likewise.

We pulled in at Corley and Kenny got the AA out on the pretence that he was travelling in the Escort with us. They looked at it and said three cylinders had gone and the choice was to be transported back or limp on although this was dangerous and the engine could pack in at any time. We could see all sorts of complications, in view of the pretence that we had got the AA out, so declined the transportation back. Kenny offered to follow us all the way back but we could not let him do that as he had already gone out of his way. He said he'd follow us until we got onto the M1, which he did. We decided to go the long way back staying on the M1 then M25 along the hard shoulder, as this was safer and better lit than cross-country via Northampton. All five of us drove in turns and we got home somewhere after two in the morning! We arranged to meet Kenny for a drink to thank him at the last game of the season, the Aston Villa match the following week. Little did I know that between now and then, I was going to get a phone call from the club telling them that I had been voted Club Superfan for the past 25 years and I was to attend a presentation on the pitch before the game.

Another of our mad away games was Stoke City in December 1984. We were travelling up in my mate Phil's Mercedes. Now when we were making the arrangements the week before, you had this picture in your mind of finally travelling to away games in style. Reality kicked in when he picked me up in Colchester on the Saturday morning. To start off with, Phil had had a heavy night at Roberts Pool club the night before and there was talk of having consumed the large part of a bottle of Southern Comfort. He needed to sleep it off so I offered to drive. It was only when I got behind the wheel that I realised the state of this old (very old) white Mercedes. From memory there was no handbrake, seatbelts nor tax and I am pretty sure that there was only one wing mirror on the passenger side. There was certainly no interior mirror or drivers side mirror. I would therefore guess there was no MOT either. Well we did the tour of the surrounding Colchester area to pick up our passengers and there were 7 of us in total. The Merc was a fairly big car but six would have been tight so seven were a nightmare, particularly with an unfit Phil first thing!

We decided to share the driving, as that was a strain in itself as there were so many bits missing. It was like Russian roulette – drive the car or sit with the other five in the back. The only comfortable seat was the front passenger one that Phil slept in for most of the way.

As we left the M6 and joined the road into Stoke, there were loads of police at the side of the road in a lay-by. This was during the Miners strikes and picketing and I believe they were there for that unless anything more interesting turned up. At that moment we did! We hammered past them and you could see their heads turn to follow our car as we went past – how many were there in the car and as they choked on the black smoke kicking out from the exhaust. We looked around and two officers were running down the lay-by to their patrol car about 50 yards away and just before we lost sight of them we could see the blue light had started to flash. We were not going to hang around to see if it was us they were interested in but as we could think of several reasons why it might be, the driver (anonymous) accelerated and reached speeds of 110 mph (Speedo could have been dodgy as well!). We kept ahead of them and could just see a blue light in the distance but they did not make much of an inroad on us. As we entered Stoke itself, we pulled off down a side street and laid low for about 20 minutes before we made our way to the ground to park. We could not swear to it being us that they had been chasing as they never got close enough but the guilty consciences made us feel like it was.

We parked on the waste land that they described as a car park at Stoke's old ground having dropped a few of our passengers off so as not to attract attention again.

Funnily enough, when we came back after the game there was a large policeman standing next to our car so we walked straight past but by the time we doubled back to it, he had gone. Just a coincidence! Phil was feeling a lot better by then and said he'd drive home so we were quite happy for him to drive his baby home as he knew it much better than his conscripted drivers did!

Liverpool away on a Bank Holiday Monday in August 1985 was also memorable as far as drinking escapades go (hence this chapter's title!). Well memorable for some, not me as the driver! The game was totally forgettable, a very inept 0-5 defeat — I believe we were 0-3 or 0-4 down within the first half an hour or so!

To cheer us up, we made a pact to go for a record number of pubs on the way home to set our away day record. We had visited one on the way up and managed another 14 on the way back south (some folk had hangovers before we made the M1). We decided to head back via Stockport and then down through the Peak District and as it was a Bank Holiday a lot of pubs had extensions until 11.30 so we achieved 15 pubs in an away trip. You might be surprised to hear that we have never beaten it! As for myself, it was interesting visiting all these pubs and it would have been nice to remember a few for future visits but it was such a rush, they were all a blurred memory and by the 10th or 12th variation on a soft drink I was really looking forward to getting home by the time we left the last pub at twenty to twelve to head for home, particularly as I was working the next day. At least I was the only one in the car that would not have a hangover!

Sixth on the list of away days by car was actually a weekend away for the thrashing of Leeds United at Elland Road in March 1989. Ipswich wiped the floor with Leeds that day but unfortunately I was with my cousin Steve who was not a great football follower and my cousin Linda's husband Vince, an ardent Leeds fan in the Gelderd End, the Leeds home end. We had Dalian Atkinson and Chris Kiwomya playing for us then and their pace just ripped the ageing slow Leeds defence apart. The 4-2 Town win flattered Leeds totally.

It really was an amazing experience knowing I was in the minority if not the only Town fan in that end but for safety's sake, I had to pretend to be disappointed. It was very difficult surging forward towards Linighan with the Leeds fans when he gave them a rude gesture but it was stand where you were and get flattened or go with the flow! When the Town third goal went in my cousin's husband gave me a stare saying without words "keep your mouth shut if you want to get out of here in one piece!" When the fourth one went in, my cousin Steve grabbed one wrist and Vince grabbed the other cause I think they thought I was going to jump up and shout out! No chance, I was pleased but not totally stupid and did not fancy taking on 10000+ jarred off Leeds fans!

Seventh on the list was Portsmouth away in October 1989 and it was not really due to the game at Fratton Park but the one beforehand in the morning. I made my debut for the Town Supporters Club and wore the number that one of my all time heroes, Paul Mariner had worn, the number 9.

We had to leave at six thirty in the morning, as it was a ten thirty kick off and we had to find the recreation ground we were playing in. It was a very windy and wet October morning as we parked up having finally found the venue. We got changed and set off for our pitch, there were 7 or 8 pitches and ours was right in the middle. So with a gale blowing and it raining heavily on and off we kicked off. It was a great honour wearing Mariner's old shirt number and the reason for that was that our captain was asking everyone where they normally played. I did not normally play anywhere so I said up front as I have always been a bit of a glory hunter so that was how I got to wear the number 9 of Town! I have always been a bit slow and did not move more than I had to. I was probably one of the few not to be frustrated every time the ball got kicked into touch because of the position of our pitch and the wind; the ball ran for what seemed like miles. The game got held up time and time again! At least I could get my breath back!

As luck would have it, I was between the penalty spot and the six-yard box when the ball broke through a ruck of players and with the goalkeeper on the floor, I had all but an empty net to aim at. I did not hit it perfectly but it rolled into the bottom of the net and turned out to be a vital contribution in a 3-2 (I believe from memory or was it 2-1 victory?) I know we won by a goal any way. In the past I maybe exaggerated by about 25 yards and 50 mph the quality and pace of the goal but the truth is finally told and I have still scored for the Tractor Boys after all! A small report even made it into the Green Un (local football paper) afterwards! We had a drink with the Portsmouth lads afterwards which was nice as I have been there several times and it is usually quite an intimidating place to visit.

Port Vale away, January 1st 1990 was a totally forgettable away trip. I had stayed sober New Year's Eve at a Party and threw friends we had staying overnight out at seven thirty so we could get there in good time. There were no other mugs on the road and we got to the ground by eleven thirty. I don't know if anyone has been to Port Vale before but there is nothing to do there at the best of times and certainly not on a Bank Holiday. Sharon and I just sat in the car until we met the player's coach at one thirty to pick up our complimentaries.

Now I am glad we had free tickets, as this was the worst performance I can ever remember (it even eclipsed 0-9 at Old Trafford) (see further on in this chapter). We were 4-0 down with still a lot of the game left and I remember a lot of people that had travelled by coach leaving after an hour or so and going to sit on the coach as they had had enough!

The bribery for Sharon was that we would find a nice country pub on the way home but that did not materialise either as we sat for four hours plus on the M6 and M1 – the best I could do was a Little Chef on the Northampton Ring road five minutes before closing!

Not Sharon's idea of reward! Needless to say, I have never stayed sober since on New Year's Eve because of the "MUST" of travelling to an Away game the next day. Once bitten, twice shy!

My next away game for the Supporter's Club was Oldham Athletic away and the thrill was actually playing at Boundary Park (as this was in the days of the artificial pitch).

The alleged main game was another pitiful performance by the Town players and they endured a 4-1 defeat. The only positive was that we had to go to the far side of the ground after 80 minutes where the community changing rooms were so we missed the last 10 minutes!

I would describe the supporters match as the main match of the afternoon that day and we ran out onto that awful surface straight after Full Time of the supposed professional game. I would guess, maybe a couple of hundred fans stayed behind to watch and we put up a much better performance than our counterparts and fought out a hard earned 3-3 draw. The thing that stands out in our memory was a couple or three of the Town players walking out to the end of the tunnel to see what was going on. They must have stayed for all of a minute before they turned round to go back down the tunnel when one of our big defenders ran to the touch line and made comments that they should stay and watch as we were far cheaper (in actual fact, FREE) to watch than them and were putting up a much better performance! They did turn round and stay and watch for another five minutes or so as a token gesture before, no doubt heading for a much more inviting and warmer players bar than a cold night in February in Oldham watching us!

I was not as lucky in front of that goal and was substituted early in the second half but at least I had appeared on a league ground. My cousin's husband Vince also made a guest appearance as a 6' 6" central defender and managed to shred not only his tracksuit bottoms but also his knees on that awful plastic pitch. I was not sorry to hear that they had gone back to grass a year or two later, however, it was with mixed feelings as if it had been a grass pitch, there was no way I would have made an appearance on the pitch at a league ground. Our match would have been somewhere similar to that of Portsmouth but no doubt a lot colder on a Saturday February evening in February. The Oldham lads were great hosts at a local pub afterwards and laid on some good grub for us. I was glad we only had to travel back to Bradford that night, as it would have been an awful long journey back to Essex on the Saturday night.

Tenth on the list was a midweek league fixture at Middlesbrough in April 1990. Sharon and I decided to make a couple of days of it and we stayed overnight before the match just outside Durham. We spent the day of the match looking round the Metro centre at Gateshead (a trade off – shopping for Sharon / football for me).

Needless to say, there were very few Town fans and I had arranged to get our complimentaries off Johnny Wark. He gave me a bundle of about 25 tickets and said to hand them around! The trouble was that there was so few and most had tickets – I just could not get rid of them all. I still had 10 or 12 in my pocket as we entered the ground! We had the back row of seats in the main stand and were separated by an empty row and some police and stewards. It was very intimidating and we left 15 minutes from the end and sat in some empty seats further along the stand in case there was any bother.

Eleventh on the list was Grimsby away in September 1991 and Sharon and I, stayed up in Bradford with Vince and Linda on the

Saturday night. Warky again came up with the tickets and I just went with big Vince. Unfortunately, these tickets were not with the away fans but in the main stand and Town won 2-1. I completely forgot myself and leapt up for both goals. The Grimsby fans are quite tough up there and I am sure we would have got lynched but I think they saw the size of Vince and as they did not know he was really a gentle giant, they left us alone apart from one nice chap giving me a kick in the back of the legs as we left the ground. It was nice to get back to the car and away.

Southend United away in April 1992, which was in the season we won the old Second division to get promotion into the new Premiership, was also an unforgettable day. I went down to this game with my old neighbour Tony who was a passionate Southend fan. Despite being the only Southend fan in the car he had bought tickets for all of us in the Southend main stand which was to prove interesting later!

The wives spent the day together and the plan was to make it a bit of an alcoholic fuelled day (the football supporters – not the wives!) but I was not bargaining on Tony knowing a pub in Rayleigh that would open up for him at quarter to ten. By the time we got to the ground we were pretty hammered! There was lots of stick and banter going on when they scored and when we did and I believe, Warky missed a penalty and we got loads of stick from the Southend fans around us. We did have the last laugh though as Neil Thompson cut in from left and hit a curler with his right foot. I remember thinking that he only used his right foot to stand on as it hit the back of the net. We celebrated albeit a bit reservedly as there had already been a fairly serious fight in front of us down near the front and a lot of known Ipswich troublemakers had been thrown out so we certainly did not want another fight starting due to us.

We headed back to the Crown at Brantham for a night of drinking (celebrating from my point of view and commiserating from Tony's!). We only made it until quarter past seven and then rang our other halves to pick us up. I blamed it on starting drinking so early in the day at Rayleigh – I am bad enough after a lunchtime session, let alone a breakfast session but I think the real truth was that I was just a lightweight when it came to serious drinking!

Oxford United away in the season we went back to the big time, 25th April 1992 was one of the highlights of away games by car as we clinched that crucial point needed in a 1-1 draw. It was a good atmosphere, which was nearly impossible at the Manor Ground due to no roof in the away end. Everyone was listening to radios for the other results which had the normal affect of causing lots of rumours and counter rumours as always happens on such occasions. I think Middlesbrough and Leicester games were the results that mattered and at the final whistle we knew we had done it. As the whistle went, hundreds poured on from the away end but we were in a tiny little stand with seats to one side of the pitch and a jobs worth steward was not letting us on through the gate. I tried reasoning with him but he was having none of it so I went over the fence and ran down the side to open another gate and everyone flooded onto the pitch. I fully admit that it was a bit of a rebellious thing to do and that the steward was only doing his job but this was a celebration we should all have been allowed to join in and as there was hundreds on the pitch already, another 100 or so from our area would make no difference. The Oxford fans were very sporting and I saw no trouble. Sharon stayed in the stand with a couple of our friends and

I met her afterwards, as she was not so keen to accompany me onto the pitch! I cannot imagine why!

Blackburn Rovers away in the Premiership on 7th May 1994 was the only match that I was physically sick afterwards through nothing to do with drink! It was the crucial game for survival and we were staying at Linda and Vince's in Bradford with Linda and Neil as well. Vince, Neil and I went to the game in good time and hit a couple of pubs but already I was feeling really tense and a bit unwell – I had a shandy in the first pub and a coke in the second just down the road from the ground. Thousands of Town fans had made the journey north and we hung on against all odds to pick up a point that we needed to have any chance of staying up. This was no mean feat cause Blackburn were a good side then. What was absolutely awful was that the draw meant Sheffield United had to lose at Chelsea or we would be down. The last we had heard was 2-2 with two minutes to go (this was about five minutes after our full time because although all games were meant to kick off at same time there had been a delay). There were a lot of long faces when suddenly the away end erupted (we had all stayed behind to listen to radios) – Mark Stein had put Chelsea 3-2 up. If they could hold on we were safe. There was another three or four minutes injury time and the tension was unbearable but Chelsea did the business and we were safe.

As we left the ground, I had an awful headache and felt sick and as we hit the motorway away from Blackburn, we pulled onto the hard shoulder and I was dreadfully sick!

We got back to Bradford and were having a Chinese Banquet take away to celebrate but I just lay on the sofa feeling awful and happy as well. The women did not believe that it was just due to the tension of the game rather than drink but it was and that is how bad football can get you sometimes!

Another memory from my away games by car was for all the wrong reasons. It was Leeds United away in the Premiership in February 1995. Neil and I were travelling up to meet Vince, my cousin Linda's husband and his mate Steve. Vince had arranged tickets in the Leeds end as usual!

I had taken delivery of a brand new Volvo that week and it had less than 100 miles on the clock when we set off. We picked Vince and Steve up in Bradford and then headed for a well-known Leeds pub not too far from the ground. We stayed in there until about twenty past two and then headed down the road to the ground thinking we were going to get parked up close to the ground as there were not many other cars parked. We had Radio 5 live on and an announcement came across stating that there was one Premiership casualty due to the weather – yes you guessed it "Leeds United v Ipswich!" As we had tickets in the Leeds stand and would not be returning for the evening game, we queued up in the pouring rain for half an hour to get a refund. We did get a glimpse of the pitch and bits were saturated and under water but it was an awful long way to get all the way there for no football.

We took Vince and Steve back to Bradford, turned a chilli down and headed off home about half past three. We rang home from Grantham and said that we'd pick up a Chinese Take Away to be greeted with no sympathy at all (or so it seemed) from Sharon who made the comment "never mind, normally when you are on the way home you have just seen them let several goals in so this was better than normal (this was the year they got relegated from the

Premiership and how true was Sharon to be proven, as soon as our next away trip!)

This next away trip was to be one of the low points of all time as an Ipswich Town supporter; it was the 0-9 defeat at Manchester United. Where do I start?! The day started well with a visit to the Manchester United museum, which was really interesting even though we were not United supporters. They are a club of great tradition and success and the museum did them proud. Little did we know that we were about to witness what is now probably one of the exhibits now!

We were absolutely pummelled that day and various records went – Andy Cole was first player to score five goals, United got record ever Premiership victory and probably one or two others! The Town support was brilliant from start to finish – just over 2000 of us, and it felt like we made as much noise as the Manchester United fans. There were some humorous moments – there had to be – manic celebrations when we won a throw on for one. The big disappointment was the players attitude at the end – ok they must have been well disappointed but what about us – we were still supporting and singing for them at the end and they walked off at the end without so much as an acknowledgement – that was well out of order. A lot of people work very hard to earn enough money to follow them all over the country and those highly paid posers should have remembered that that day above any disappointment that they might have been feeling. You have to give the Manchester United fans their due – they stayed behind to applaud the Town fans that day for their support and I will always appreciate that. It would have been nice if the Town players had remembered to as well! As we left the ground, we chatted to some United fans from Norwich of all places who said that Town Supporters deserved a better team than that in view of the way they supported them.

We stopped off at Corley service area on the M6 on the way home and chatted with a few more United fans (they all wanted to talk to us that day – cannot imagine why!). I spoke to this old girl decked out from head to foot in Manchester United scarves, badges, rosettes etc. She was the spitting image of Bet Lynch off Coronation Street and was very gobby about the result. I remember saying to her that I thought the ref was biased and that if he had disallowed Paul Ince's quick free kick whilst Craig Forrest was still arguing that the result could have been different. She really took exception to this and went on and on at me until I pointed out that I was winding her up, as we were 6-0 down at the time! This result certainly went to show that Sharon's observation about the Leeds game that never was, was a better result than we were usually treated to that season!

Last on the car journeys was Derby County away on 19th May 2001. This was an amazing match; just down to the position we were in going into the match. This was Town's first season back in the Premiership after Wembley 2000 and against all the odds, they were going into the last away game at Derby in a cannot lose situation. Win and depending on other results, they would be in the Champions League, draw or lose and they would be in the UEFA Cup – the Tractor Boys were in Europe. It was a carnival atmosphere with thousands of Tractor Boys and Girls (this was the season that the Tractor Boys name really stuck) making the trip to the Midlands to celebrate. A 1-1 draw saw them qualify for the UEFA Cup which would have been the case had they won due to other results so we were pleased to be there to witness the end to a brilliant season. In hindsight, I think qualifying for Europe happened too soon and left us there to be shot at the following year and we all know what happened then. But who would have swapped those experiences in places like Helsingborg and Milan?

CHAPTER 6

UEFA CUP WINNERS AND I WAS THERE

My first experience of Europe was an unbeatable atmosphere in the Seventies under the lights at Portman Road. Who could forget the balmy nights of beating such greats as Barcelona with Cruyff and Co. But it was not just the big boys that resulted in the atmosphere – there seemed to be a magic whoever we played on our many European nights whether it was in the UEFA Cup or the old European Cup Winners Cup. Maybe that magical atmosphere has contributed to the Tractor Boys still being the only English Team that is unbeaten at home in over 40 years of competitive European Football.

These tasters led me to looking forward to travelling abroad with Town. In those days it was not that simple as it was not so easy to jump on a flight and be there in an hour or two as it would be nowadays (even that is not so simple nowadays though, as I hate flying and apart from Pre Season, we are nowhere near Europe anymore!).

My most memorable experiences of European away days was during the never to be forgotten UEFA Cup winning season of 1980 / 81. It was my first full year in work as a 16 year old and my holiday that year was to be used up following Town away in Europe from the Quarter Finals onwards.

The trips were as follows:

St Etienne away – The Quarter Finals:

Nigel, John and I were three of a handful of supporters that travelled down to St Etienne independently by train. We met at Victoria on the Tuesday night and caught the boat train down to Dover. We then sailed to Dunkerque and after a couple of hours sleep in a waiting room at Dunkerque Port railway station, we caught a train to Paris in the early hours of Wednesday morning. We then travelled across Paris on the Metro to catch a train south in mid morning for the 5-hour journey to St Etienne. When we arrived at the departure point, there were special trains leaving every half an hour or so laid on for the Paris based St Etienne fans. In those days, St Etienne were one of the top teams in France and their supporters were fanatical, thinking nothing of doing the near 1000 mile round trip South and back to support their team.

The train we got was an ordinary SNCF train but even that still had quite a few St Etienne fans on it and we got chatting to some friendly opposition supporters. They told us that they did the trip for every home game and it was worth it, as they never lost! They said that whilst they admired our dedication, we were wasting our time, as they had never lost a home European tie in over 20 years. We told them that there had to be a first and that today, it would happen.

We arrived in St Etienne late afternoon and headed straight for the ground. Upon arriving at the ground, there were a good number of Town fans that had taken various duration coach trips. We bumped into the Town Directors who were doing a walk around mixing outside the ground and just generally enjoying the build up to the game.

Town had looked after the official supporters first who mostly had tickets on the terracing behind one goal to the side. We had no choice but to shell out for expensive seats that were at the diagonal opposite end of the ground. There were not many Town fans in that part of the ground so we hoisted up our Union Jack and gave a loud (but not tuneful) rendition of God Save the Queen. There were soon boos, whistles and cat calls from the home fans and then a few coins and bottles rained down in our direction so we ended up prematurely ending our song as requested by a grumpy gendarme. (I am not sure if they objected to our attempt at being patriotic or our lack of tune!)

Despite the long journey, even the most optimistic amongst us gave us little or no chance of even a draw away to St Etienne.

How wrong could we be – Ipswich had no regard for reputation or unbeaten home records that night and they totally dismantled that proud unbeaten European home record despite going a goal down early on. A team with players such as Michel Platini, Johnny Rep and Johnny Metgod were thrashed 4-1 in the greatest ever Ipswich performance in my opinion. We were in the Semi Finals without even needing to worry about the second leg at Portman Road in a fortnight.

During the game we had befriended an English couple, who were English teachers and lived in that area of France. The husband followed Ipswich from afar so it was a dream come true for him not only that they were playing on his doorstep but the way they demolished the local team as well (I am sure he held his head up high at work the next day!).

As we left the ground, they said to cover our colours up as the locals could be unpleasant, (this was a shame to do after such a result but common sense and self preservation prevailed!). They offered to give the three of us a lift back to the railway station which we gratefully accepted. They had omitted to say that they only had a small mini. It was quite a squeeze getting three of us in the back and I am sure Nigel won't mind me saying that he would have fitted the back quite comfortably by himself but we managed it! We said our thanks and farewells at the station.

We kept our colours hidden until we were about to climb onto the night train bound for Paris that departed at some time after 11pm. All of a sudden there was a shout of "Hey – Engleesh boys – look what we have for you!" We dreaded to imagine and were waiting for the punch up but we had nothing to fear. It was the St Etienne fans that we had travelled down with on the train south earlier in the day. They had bought a crate of Heineken for us to share with them on the way north. Lots of drinking and mutual teaching of French and English football songs and swear words ensued and we were much the worse for wear when we pulled into Paris just after 5 a.m. on the Thursday morning.

We managed to find a café open within view of the Eiffel Tower at 6.30 a.m. and had freshly baked croissants with a bottle of champagne to celebrate!

We caught the train back to the Hoverport at Calais where we were booked onto a Hovercraft for the journey back across the Channel. After several more beers by the time we left the hovercraft, we managed to leave a St Etienne flag, couple of scarves and a small camera on it and we never did get them back!

Cologne away – The Semi Finals

Following our safe second leg at Portman Road, Ipswich were drawn against Cologne or 1FC Koln in the UEFA Cup Semi Finals. With the first leg won 1-0 at Portman Road, it set us up for the second leg nicely which we had had to book up before the first leg was played.

Amazingly, in those days, the Football League did little to assist the English Teams playing in Europe and we were playing at Norwich in the Local Derby on the Easter Monday before the second leg on the Wednesday. You could not get much worse preparation, having had a game on the Saturday and then losing at Norwich 48 hours before the match in Germany. That fixture scheduling would just not happen nowadays.

Anyway, I remember watching the game at Carrow Road on the Monday. Work during the day on the Tuesday and then catching the night ferry from Harwich to The Hook of Holland on the Tuesday night. We then got the boat train from the Hook on the Wednesday morning that took us directly to Cologne, which was one of the stops on the train's journey down to Munich.

Cologne was a lovely city; good sights, food and beer and we were booked into a small hotel near the cathedral in the centre. What more could a football supporter want? The only downside was that the stadium was a long way out from the centre. We caught a tram or trolley bus out to the ground and there were several thousand Town fans boosted by a large presence of German based British squaddies supporting the English team who had all turned up in their khaki army buses. I would say that the total support for Town including the squaddies was between 3000 – 5000, which was great numbers for the early 80s when travel was not as straightforward as today. The squaddies enjoyed goading the German police and Cologne supporters during the game which sprung to life well into the second half when Terry Butcher scored a late winner to take us into the final.

What I most remember about after the match was the speed that not only the squaddies' buses but the official supporters coaches departed afterwards leaving us "unofficials" to make our way back into the centre of Cologne and it was not a particularly pleasant walk back. The Germans were after blood and it was a long walk back. (We had seen a couple of incidents on the trams / trolley buses going back straight after the match so walking seemed the lesser of two evils!). Luckily I had swapped scarves before the match so I had a red 1FC Koln scarf, which I put on, and as we walked the last stretch into the centre, by then we had seen several scuffles and fights as Ipswich fans were targeted by Germans.

As we had got near to the Centre after about half an hour walking, a group of Ipswich fans that had been on the receiving end came towards us – we had to rapidly let them know who we were as they appeared to be ready to dish out some retaliation!

We were glad to get back into the safety of the hotel and we decided that would be the safest place for a few beers that night. There were quite a few Town fans sleeping in the open and stories we heard the next day indicated that most had to keep on the move all night or make their way into the main railway station where there was a police presence for their own safety.

The next day we picked up the boat train back to the Hook and we were greeted by loads of scousers heading back from the European Cup Semi final victory over Bayern Munich. Victory had put them in a mood for a joint celebration with us. European success was nothing new to them but it was a new and enjoyable experience for us and they were happy to celebrate with us.

In the carriage that we joined, there was this scouser in a pair of Y fronts and two different trainers shoes and nothing else. We soon got into his story and apparently, he had got trollied the night before and fallen asleep on a park bench so when he woke up all he had left was his pants – everything else including his mates had gone (I suppose he was lucky that his pants remained – we certainly were!). He was still unsure whether it had been Germans or his mates but he had lost almost everything. He had got in with some others who had nicked him trainers albeit differing ones from a couple of sports shops but that was as far as they had got as they made dash for and caught the boat train. He was now getting worried as he had lost his ticket and passport. We made a collection of clothes so attention was not drawn to him. He got a pair of tracksuit bottoms and an old jumper and I was all heart and donated him a pair of socks! I don't know if he looked much better as the bottoms were several sizes too big but he did look less conspicuous! I am still not quite sure how he got past Customs and Ticket control without a passport or ticket but I think his mates planned to push through in a big group with him in the middle. It must have worked as we saw him on the ferry later during the crossing. I don't know what happened to him when we arrived at Harwich!

It sounded like it had been amazingly easy to get him on board (it's amazing the asylum seekers don't try that scam nowadays!).

On the boat train back to the Hook, we had also met a lad called Pete and his sister who were from Lincoln and were returning to England after a backpacking tour around Europe. We got chatting and he loved the atmosphere on the train and said he fancied going to the final to support us if we could get him a ticket even though he was not really into football. I subsequently managed to and he travelled out to Amsterdam in our group for the final.

AZ67 in Amsterdam – The Final

The last of my UEFA Cup winning adventures that year was the UEFA Cup Final 2nd Leg. Town had won the first leg at home 3-0 and all was set up for a major celebration at and after the return leg. It was, however, not far off going all wrong but we always looked like we would hang on once we got an away goal, ending up losing 4-2 on the night but winning 5-4 on aggregate. So after that long season of over 60 games, Town had finally won something – they were a great team that year and it would have been very unjust if they had won nothing after losing out on the league to Villa and in the FA Cup Semi Finals to Manchester City.

Ipswich took about 8000 supporters and AZ67 Alkmaar being a club with a small ground elected to play the second leg at the Olympic Stadium in Amsterdam.

We travelled over on one of the several chartered ferries from Harwich to Hook of Holland (It had been handy living in Dovercourt that year!) One big alcoholic fuelled party ensued. Sealink tried to improve their profit margins by hiking the price of drinks in the bars on the ferry so we resorted to using the corkscrew I had in my rucksack and buying bottles of wine from the duty free as the beer ran out quick as it was a cheaper alternative to the bars. I remember seeing Brian Talbot, the ex Ipswich player (then with Arsenal) and friends and they'd had quite a bit to drink too – so much in fact, I believe they left their car in the Hook and travelled up to Amsterdam by train instead!

We had a hotel close to the Red Light district and our group had four rooms for two people each.

After the match, we made our way back to the Red Light district, as that was where everyone was heading to for a drink to celebrate. There was drinking, singing and general partying and even a massive conga which must have had 500 or more Town fans going down one side of the canal, over a little bridge back up the other side and then over another little bridge (some even fell in the canal but no-one cared – we were winners!).

There were also the shop windows where all the ladies of the night plied their trade – tonight they were also displaying Ipswich or AZ67 scarves to boast their success or lack of it! I don't know if their customers got discount if they let them keep the scarf? The party went on until around five in the morning before we made our way back to the hotel. I would hasten to add that I had happily spent the night simply sipping beer after beer celebrating. I had never been one to enjoy any type of shopping and that type of window-shopping certainly did not appeal for one moment!

We were not going to get more than two or three hours sleep but we were at least some of the lucky ones that had booked accommodation to go back to – I know a lot didn't. Anyway, as we made our way back, we met up with about 20 or so fans that we knew, who did not have accommodation so we let them come back to our hotel and let them in through the fire exits – people were sleeping everywhere. One lad was in our bath and his mates thought the best alarm call he could have as he was pretty hung over was to start the taps the next morning– he was not happy as he only had one set of clothes that he'd still been in.

We would have got away with it until about 30 people went down for breakfast from rooms that held eight at eight thirty. We slipped the waitress some guilders and she did not make a fuss.

The UEFA Cup run had certainly been a great way to spend my first year's holiday from work and I could not wait for the next European Tour.

CHAPTER 7

EUROPEAN PRE-SEASON TOURS

My actual first experience of following Town into Europe was nearly two years earlier than the UEFA Cup winning run and was in August 1979 when I went with a mate Kevin to watch Town in the Fejenoord Tournament in Rotterdam in Holland. We stayed with Frieda, a friend of my parents in The Hague and travelled to and from Rotterdam by train (even in those days, Dutch trains were top class – clean and on time without fail). We bought tickets for the whole tournament and you watched two matches on one day (the semis) and then the third place and final, two days later. Town beat PSV Eindhoven (no bad result) 3-1 in their semi and Fejenoord disposed of RWD Molenbeek from Belgium so it was Fejenoord v Ipswich final. We had excellent front row seats just to the side of one of the goals and were looking forward to sitting in the same seats for the final. When we got back to The Hague, Frieda's brother was very excited, as he had seen us on the television several times.

The final, two days later was a marvellous match with Town just being edged out 5-4 but it was one of those games that you did not really mind losing as it was so exciting (and was only a pre-season tournament after all!). Frieda's brother reported that we had been seen a further few times on the television that day and the final had been live on Dutch TV. It had been an enjoyable first experience of European Tours and we found the Dutch lovely hosts then and have done each time we have visited Holland since.

My next European Tour, UEFA Cup winning year aside, was to cover the pre-season tour of Scandinavia in August 1983 and I have some great memories from it.

I left Harwich on the DFDS ferry for Esbjerg with my mate Ray Slegg and one of his mates and we were the only three supporters to follow Town from England that year. We drove the length of Denmark to pick up a further ferry across to Sweden, as the direct sailing to Sweden did not fit in with the first game.

The first game was away to Fredrikstad, just over the Norwegian border from Sweden and I remember having my photo taken with Russell Osman and Terry Butcher outside the player's hotel before the game.

The day after followed a game with Lillestroem further up into Norway and then we had a mammoth journey right along the south coast of Norway to Stavanger on the South Western most tip of Norway.

I think we were becoming celebrities amongst the opposition fans and even with the Town players, as we were the only three supporters following Town all over Norway in my mark 1 Vauxhall Cavalier (we did several thousand miles and I still don't know how it survived!).

I remember approaching a toll barrier as we drew closer to Stavanger and it was one of these sorts with a bucket that you had to throw the money in. As we were driving on the Right, the responsibility was therefore, down to the front passenger who had a handful of change but missed the bucket with some of it. We had no more change and got out to retrieve it but as we had caused quite a jam, a big Norwegian came and topped our contribution up so that the jam would clear! He obviously thought his contribution would be a less painful option than waiting for us English idiots to sort ourselves out!

Anyway, we made it to the Viking Stavanger ground (Chelsea fans will remember it where they lost last year!). We saw the team arrive and I don't quite know how it came about but Paul Mariner, England Centre Forward at the time said let's have a kick about referring to the plastic ball we had with us for a kick around before the game. So we ended up having a kick around in the road outside the ground with our hero for a few minutes and had our photo to capture the moment. What was even better was the invite Paul gave us to go back to the Team hotel after the match and have a meal with them as thanks for our support. The match was of little consequence with that to look forward to afterwards!

Kick about in the road with England No9 Paul Mariner, Ray
Slegg and myself

After the match we followed the Team Coach back to the team
hotel and were ushered into a big restaurant where there was a
magnificent hot and cold buffet laid on for the team (and us)!
Halfway through the meal, the hotel staff working that evening all

came in and asked for autographs – when they got to me it was a bit embarrassing but Paul Mariner said "Go on sign – you are one of the reserves!" I did and could be accused of impersonation or pretending to be one of the players. Ray had a bit more decency about him although even in those days he would never have got away as even a veteran! I did wonder afterwards if they ever worked out who Graeme Brooke was. We then went with the players downstairs to the hotel nightclub and had a few beers and were not allowed to buy a drink all night. It was a great gesture and really appreciated.

The next day we caught the ferry north across the fjord from Stavanger and despite it being in August, it was one of the roughest crossings that I have experienced and I am a good sailor. I would hate to experience that crossing in the winter! It was a bit windy but not that strong and I understood that the extremely deep channels had something to do with it. Luckily I had left my car parked in gear but the Norwegians either side hadn't and they'd rolled slightly into each other with minor damage (broken side lights / indicators etc) and this was only August.

We were pleased to get off the ferry and leave it behind as we made our way along a beautiful road between mountains and Fjords as we headed back towards Oslo (several hundred miles away). I still think Norway is one of the most scenic countries if not the best that I have been to.

As the road climbed through one mountain range, there was snow right up to the edge of the road so we stopped for an impromptu snowball fight and obligatory photo. Well, no one would believe that we could have had a snowball fight in August. We refrained from making a snowman and were soon on our way again. Quite amazing though for early August.

We had a spare bit of time before heading back for the ferry and spent an enjoyable few hours in Oslo visiting the Bislet stadium where Sebastian Coe and Steve Ovett had broken world records and then enjoyed a few hours at an open air café enjoying a beer or two. The amazing thing was that, we were sitting in temperatures in the eighties, less than 24 hours after having a snowball fight a couple of hundred miles away.

It was then time to head south for Gothenburg to catch the ferry back to Harwich on the late Sunday afternoon. We were at the port in good time, as we simply could not afford to miss the ferry as we had a deadline to meet – the ferry was due back in Harwich at six o'clock the following Monday afternoon. So what you might say but we were clockwatching, hoping that there would be no delay as that night, it was George Burley's testimonial with Aberdeen.

Luckily the ferry was in time but by the time we got through Customs, it was gone half past six so I did not have time to call in at home in Dovercourt, a mile or so away – it was straight to Ipswich and we were inside Portman Road with 15 minutes to spare!

Well after that holiday which had been my most enjoyable one to date, my thoughts were firmly on the next pre-season tour, the following season. My mate Nick and a chap called Andy who had contacted me via the Town programme were to be my two travel companions and sadly, both of them, have since died young at the ages of 34 and 40 respectively so are no longer with us today.

It was to be quite an enjoyable trip but not a patch on the previous pre-season. Unfortunately, this was in a lot of ways down to the fact that Nick and I did not particularly get on well with Andy.

This was to be a long and tiring trip of just under three weeks, which was to cover several thousand miles. We were going to travel to both the Scandinavian leg of the tour and then onto the games in Holland, which was to form the second part of the pre–season. Whilst the players flew home for a few days break in between, we would be travelling between Scandinavia and Holland via ferry and through Denmark and Germany.

We expected there to be very few Town supporters out in Sweden and Norway based on the previous pre-season and when we made it known to the club, they gave us a load of posters and club shop catalogues to hand out at games. Anything to help the club gain more supporters and hopefully we added a few to the numbers of what is nowadays a fairly good sized Scandinavian supporters club.

I also knew Peter Slater who is now with Radio 5 but was the sports editor with Radio Orwell (to become SGR) at the time. At this time there was great competition between Radio Orwell and the East Anglian Daily Times as to who could get first details of news on Town so Peter Slater asked me if I'd mind phoning through brief reports on the games out in Scandinavia. I needed to do it on the night straight after games so that they could get it on a sports desk the next morning and it was generally a day ahead of the paper, as they did not have a reporter out there. I was thrilled to be asked so he gave me his home number and I would phone the details through after each game. That was a feat in itself as it often took quite a time to not only find a phone box but also one that took International calls (this was pre mobile phone days!). He was then going out to Holland to report and was going to meet up with us to buy us a beer as thanks – we certainly earned it.

The games were mostly pretty uneventful. We handed out the club bits and they went down so well that they'd all gone after the first couple of games in Norrstrands and Kongsvinger so if there is a concentration of Scandinavian based fans in these areas but not so much in Ludvika and Orje you will now know why.

The friendly with Norrstrands was played in the Swedish Lakeside town of Karlstad and the next game was in Kongsvinger, just over the Norwegian border. The Kongsvinger game was quite special as we managed to get both teams to stand on the Half Way Line for Team Photos.

It was funny after the Kongsvinger game because by this time we were just about on exploding point with Andy so Nick and I went out on a pedallo at the camp site late at night leaving Andy on the beach drinking the beer (we took some with us). We really slagged him off before we came back in from a long way out. When we got back in we sat on the beach and Andy was a bit distant with us and it was only when some other campers went out on a pedallo and were talking that we realised how far the talking travelled – he must have heard every word!

Later on that night was our experience of "WOLVES" and I mean the four-legged variety, not those from Molineux! Well wolves, according to Andy. We had two ridge tents – Nick and I shared one and Andy had his own ancient scouting tent, complete with wooden poles. Every time we arrive at a campsite (and there were quite a few on that tour), it took Andy three times as long to put it up as mine and Nick's more modern tent and he would not be helped. We'd then cook a meal and Andy would accuse us of not dividing the food up fairly and so it went on like that for the whole holiday.

Anyway, back to the wolf. At about 1 a.m. on the night after the Kongsvinger game, we heard Andy screaming as he leapt about in his tent shouting, "Wolf" and trying to get into ours! Now we were fairly confident there wasn't one as we were not that far north in Norway and they do not normally approach humans. We also remembered that the campsite owner's ancient Alsatian did tend to enjoy a wander around the site the previous evening. By this time Andy's ancient tent had collapsed with him half in and half out. After enjoying (if you could at that time of night) Andy's spectacle, we looked over and he was still trying to get untangled – still half in and half out of the tent. I think he would have brought that in with him to our tent if he could of. We eventually calmed him down but could not convince him that 1. It was not a wolf and 2. if it had been, it would have been frightened miles away by now. Bearing in mind how long he normally took to put his tent up and it was the early hours of the morning, I suggested to him that he slept in the back of the Capri, and locked the doors so that the wolf could not get him!

The next morning, the story unfolded how Andy had seen a shadow of the giant Wolf sniffing around the entrance to his tent. Once the mess was tidied up, the remains of Andy's dinner was found next to his plate so the real version was more likely that despite Andy's continual complaint that we never shared the dinner out properly, he had more than he could cope with and that the campsite owner's ancient Alsatian fancied an extra snack on his leftovers. The lesson learnt was that Andy was not only getting his fair share but more than he could manage and he certainly was not so greedy after that although he was still convinced that he had been visited by wolves!

We left the campsite by nine the next morning after a somewhat interrupted night for the long journey across Sweden. As we left, we happened to see the owners Wolf (sorry – Alsatian) asleep at the exit – obviously sleeping off the midnight feast. Nick started shouting, "it's a Wolf, It's a wolf" which did not go down well with Andy. His tent was never quite the same after that brush with wildlife with one pole snapped so the tent that never looked quite right to start with now had big sag in the middle of the roof due to the broken pole.

The journey across Northern Sweden was another experience with a journey of approximately 400 miles to Ludvika in the east. We thought that it would be a relatively comfortable journey of some 400 miles over two days but we had not reckoned on the fact that although it showed as a main red road on the map, the reality was that upwards of seventy five percent of its length was on an unmade camber i.e. dirt and gravel as opposed to tarmac through the Northern forests of Sweden. If I was Colin Macrae, the rally driver, it would have been great fun but for the journey we had to undertake, apart from the scenery, it was truly awful. Even the scenery got boring after a time – when you have seen one pine tree, you have seen a hundred of them! There were quite a few signs for reindeer but none for wolves though!

It was two very long days driving but we made it and met up with Phil, Dave and Christine, the other car load, who had opted not to travel to Kongsvinger but go straight from Karlstad to Ludvika. There was also a chap from Boxford or maybe it was Boxted who was following Town by bus and train. They said their roads were much better and could not believe the ones we had experienced. At least we would travel back on those roads and not back the way that we had come.

Another unmemorable game in footballing terms (pre-season games often are) but we got some good souvenir photos with various players before kick off.

Nick, Terry Butcher and me before the Ludvika game

After that it was off to a very remote town back on the Swedish and Norwegian border called Orje.

Big Phil decided that he was going to take advantage of the hot evening and at one end of the ground there was a river that you could walk down to so he decided on a bit of impromptu skinny dipping inside the ground and we have a photo with him and his Ipswich bag being the only thing covering up his modesty! I don't suppose there can be that many people around the world that can lay claim to skinny-dipping inside a football stadium once they have gone through the turnstiles but Phil certainly could.

Following the game, the Orje supporters invited us to go to their supporters club bar for a drink which we readily accepted as we had ran out of our own supplies by now and bars in Scandinavia appeared to be in very limited supply and also very expensive.

We expected to go to another part of the ground but as this was little more than a park pitch, it involved following this old boy in a Volvo (they all drive them in Scandinavia) and heading back into the suburbs of Orje. We eventually got to an apartment block on a small housing estate, parked up and followed them in. On the first floor was what looked like a normal flat but it had been converted into a supporters club and shrine to the local club. The conversation was patchy as they could only speak Basic English and we could not speak their language at all. It sounded like this was an unofficial venue that the local police turned a blind eye to, as they and all the other residents were all members! I could have that totally wrong but I think that was what they said. Anyway, we made our excuses and left our hospitable friends behind and headed back to the campsite about 2 a.m. as we had a the long drive down south to the bottom tip of Sweden later that morning and then onto Copenhagen via the ferry where we would stop off for a couple of nights en route to Holland for the second leg of the pre-season tour. I am not sure what happened to Phil, Dave and Christine but we would meet up with them again at a campsite in Holland.

Later that day we drove onto the ferry to cross to Denmark, which was across a short strait, and we were being guided onto the ferry when I hit the side of the ferry. I thought it looked close but trusted the crew hands judgement as he obviously guided people onto the ferry all the time. I went loopy at the sight of the scraped paintwork down the side of my beautiful Capri and walked back round to the open driver's door. Just at this moment as he was manoeuvring himself out of the back seat to get out, Andy came out with a classic that he could have told me that I was going to hit the side of the ferry. I flipped and slammed the door and walked off, but unfortunately Andy's leg was half out and it slammed on him. That gave him something else to moan about and he just never knew when to stop! At that point if Nick had not calmed me down, I think Andy may well have been swimming to Denmark!

We arrived in Copenhagen and after some fun with navigating through and around the city, got to the campsite. We had chosen one on the outskirts near a railway station to allow us easy access to the city centre without the car the next day.

The next day, we got a train into the centre and headed straight for the Carlsberg factory. Had to get our priorities right as far as sightseeing goes! We were soon on a guided tour of the factory, which was interesting, but we were already looking forward to the sampling at the end. As the tour came to an end, my plan was coming together and as we entered this large hall, the tables all had 8 – 10 seats. I made a beeline for a table with five Hindus sitting on it

– Nick could not understand why I was so keen to sit there but soon realised. None of our table was going to drink alcohol apart from the three of us. The Hindu tourists drank fruit juices so that left four trays of various samples of bottle and cans of Carlsberg. Well it would have been rude to waste it so we drank as much as we could and then put the rest into our rucksacks. All we needed to do was buy a cheap bottle opener as we forgot to take the one off the table. We were set up for the day and spent the rest of it on a boat tour seeing the Little Mermaid and then in the Tivoli Gardens and we did not buy a beer all day. It was a good day to have left the car safely at the campsite.

On with the long journey, the following day down to Northern Holland where Ipswich were playing in a tournament involving Heerenveen, Cambuur and Sporting Gijon. There was one near serious incident on the motorway in Germany when Andy let out a high-pitched scream and his leg shot through the gap between the passenger and drivers seats in the front and nearly took Nick's ear off as he was driving at the time. Andy was complaining of cramp in the bruised leg that I had shut the door on, on the ferry, a few days earlier. We pulled over so he could stretch his legs and I explained that the cure would be to cut his leg off and put it in the boot if it happened again whilst I was driving.

We camped near where the tournament was being played in Northern Holland and met up with Phil, Dave and Christine plus a charming couple – John "Bradford" Hulley and his good lady Nell. They lived in Rotterdam but despite John originating from up North, he was an ardent Town fan. We went to the games in the tournament with them all and saw Town beat Cambuur but then get thrashed 3-0 by a good Sporting Gijon team in the final.

John and Nell departed but had invited us all down to stay at their flat, a couple of days later when Town were playing near them in the South at Neeuw Lekkerland, suburb of Rotterdam.

We arrived at their flat on the day of the game and all six of the Town travellers in the two cars were to share the lounge as a bedroom so it would be cosy but we were all friends (well mostly!) Luckily, it was a very large Lounge / Diner.

We watched a 4-0 victory for Town having got to the game by bus so we could have a few beers – after all, Peter Slater did promise some (and after the fun that we had had in some places in the Scandinavian countryside, we felt we had deserved them). This was Peter's first game covering Town and we had done the same for him at the Cambuur / Heerenveen tournament albeit the phones were a lot more readily available in Holland! We met up with Peter and had a couple of beers in the social club afterwards. By this match, a coach load of Town supporters had come over from England to take this match in and the last one at Utrecht.

Back to the flat and a few more drinks and then bed. Despite the cramped surroundings (six in a room, however big it is, felt cramped to me), getting a bit of kip was relatively painless until it was just starting to get light at about 5 a.m. At this time, I heard some noises from outside and at first, I just thought it was someone going to work early but they carried on and off for a few minutes so I got up and looked around the curtain. There were three local lads with a screwdriver who had just broken a window in Dave's car and had the door open. One of them was now trying to force my car door on the Capri. In an instant, without considering any possible consequences, I was pulling on some tracksuit bottoms over my boxers and shouting at the others to get up and follow me.

Unfortunately, having just woken up, they were not quite so forward thinking. I had the flat door open and was down the corridor closely followed by the others apart from Christine. The flat was on the ground floor so we got out and halfway down the path before these local car thieves realised that they had been rumbled and fled. We chased them down the road but could not catch up, probably as we were all in bare feet and two of our group had omitted to put anything on at all (they had obviously been sleeping in the altogether!) which was quite amusing but must have been even more disturbing for the few neighbours that had got up, having been disturbed by the commotion. Probably more disturbing than the car theft was itself!

It turned out that they had had the ferry tickets out of Dave's car but had luckily dropped the passports right outside the car.

A phone call to my dad in Harwich that morning got him onto the case of sorting replacement tickets which would be left for Dave at the Hook of Holland for him to collect on the way home after the Utrecht game.

We reported the incident to the Dutch police who were sympathetic but not much help (although it served its purpose for insurance purposes in case any of us needed to claim for damage to the car etc). After this we left John and Nell who were upset about what had happened to our cars and also the fact that they could not make the Utrecht game due to John's work. Obviously they could not be blamed and it was nice to see them briefly when they visited my parent's house for a meal when they travelled through the port of Harwich en route some months later. At least a little bit of the hospitality could be returned. Thanks Mum.

We decided to stay at a hotel about 10 miles from Utrecht mainly because it had a lockable garage as Dave's car was not secure with a broken window and mine was questionable as I was not sure, how much damage had been done, if any to the central locking.

Four of us decided to get the bus back into Utrecht but Dave and Christine decided to give it a miss. We arrived late but were invited, free of charge into the main stand by some high up official of the Utrecht club. (We'd got chatting to him outside briefly and explained our lateness was due to our car woes so he looked after us well).

After the game, we bumped into fans off the supporter's coach and they said it was not full, so offered us a lift back as close as they could to our hotel without detouring into the Dutch countryside late at night. They dropped us on the slip road off the dual carriageway or motorway that led to the town or village that our hotel was in. We then walked quickly back although it took quite a while, as Andy was not that quick. It's a good job we'd got that lift, as we had no idea how we would have got back to the hotel afterwards.

Next day we made our way back to the port at Hook of Holland and the tickets were waiting for Dave's car. We had a good crossing back mixing with the coach load of supporters that had given us a lift the night before and also the team who were on the same crossing.

You may think that I am being a bit unkind and disrespectful, being critical of Andy who is now dead but the story is being told throughout this book as it happened. I think that it goes to show that going on holiday with someone that you have never met before is difficult and can be a recipe for a disaster if you don't get on really well. Anyway, Andy, the picture of your one pair of light Khaki (to start with) trousers that you wore through day and night for three weeks (apart from John and Nell's flat when you needed them on!) still brings a smile to my face despite the fact that they could have stood up by themselves at the end. I think he was saving on luggage space with clothes as his old tent took up so much room.

As I said at the start of this excerpt of my final Pre-Season European Tour, sadly, both Nick and Andy died very young (at age 34 and 40 respectively) so let's hope that they are resting in peace somewhere and not getting too depressed with the results.

CHAPTER 8

WEMBLEY 2000

This adventure started a few weeks earlier than the final itself with the Play Off semi finals against Bolton Wanderers – the big question after both legs was "How on earth were we even looking forward to that final at Wembley at the end of May 2000?"

I remember queuing up at 6 a.m. in the morning for tickets for the away leg at Bolton and ending up getting interviewed on Look East. I got asked what inspired me to be there so early in the morning and to set off even earlier on the Sunday for the match as it was a lunchtime kick off. I replied instantly that I was looking forward to watching The Tractor Boys roast Bolton whilst the only thing that Delia Smith would be roasting was her Sunday Dinner at home in her kitchen (referring to Norwich's failure to qualify again). That appeared on the local television and I got ribbed about it.

Anyway to the semis themselves – away to Bolton 2-0 down early on, injuries forcing key players to go off and our dreams all but in tatters already. But we had Marcus Stewart, a superb goal poacher. He hit two crackers and we were back in with a shout with the first leg ending 2-2 and all to play for in the second leg. Then that second leg and oh what a match – I think Big Sam had decided that the only chance Bolton would have would be to kick anything that moved but it all backfired for him and they ended up with two players getting red cards. Magilton hit that equaliser with almost the last kick in the last few seconds and then we went onto win 5-3 after extra time. It was totally the wrong tactics and Bolton could well have won it, had they tried to play football that night. But they didn't and it was the Tractor Boys that were going to Wembley.

The build up to the Play Off Final was exciting with lots of local and some national press and media coverage. I was enjoying every minute (It would not dawn on me until they had kicked off at Wembley, just how critically important this one off match was for not only the club, but the whole local community).

Did and I got to Portman Road at quarter to five in the morning to queue up for Final tickets on the day that they went on sale. I could not believe it when we arrived but there were already about 100 people in the queue and the ones nearest the front had been there since eleven o'clock for tickets that did not go on sale until nine in the morning. There was a marvellous camaraderie with flasks, sleeping bags and lots of chatter. There was the odd kick around of a ball in the street next to the queue. There were Wembley stadium maps posted all along the perimeter at Portman Road where we were queuing so by the time we got to the front of the queue, we had decided the section we wanted. It was not as simple as that as the table we had to go to was not selling tickets for that section so we settled for tickets in the same price band. We took the most expensive seats as we were determined to have a good day out. The seats turned out to be very good, near the half way line just opposite the Royal Box.

Needless to say, there was a whole group of us that wanted to travel down together so we priced up options and checked availability and settled on a minibus with driver that Did arranged as the driver was one of his neighbours.

The day arrived and so did the minibus. You can imagine my horror when I saw that it was bright Norwich Yellow! It picked me and Jim, one of my neighbours up from the end of my road. We gave Did and the driver some stick about the colour and did a quick DIY job with scarves and flags. We set off as Sharon and Rachel saw us off and I think Rachel wished she were going too. We had various pick up points in Brantham and Colchester en route to Wembley. Tony, Steve and wife, Tony and Steve's dad and wife at Brantham and they came laden with beer, cool boxes and disposable barbecues. I now realised why we had kept one free seat. We picked John and the rest up in Colchester.

We were soon on the A12 and it appeared that every car, minibus or coach was decorated in blue and white. This was to be the biggest ever following of Town supporters at one game around the 38000 mark. (although the record crowd at Portman Road for that Leeds game was 38010, (see first chapter), several thousand Leeds fans were part of it).

As we arrived on the outskirts of Wembley, the colours were stunning – bright blue or bright red, no halfway measure and it looked brilliant. Fans of both sides were mingling in the pubs – no trouble to be seen – football how it should be.

We parked up the minibus in the official Wembley car and coach park and nipped off to find a pub for a couple of pints, then it was back to the minibus. Tony had kindly taken on the Chef's role and was doing a sterling job. It had been a great idea of his because one of the major drawbacks of Wembley is how the catering and merchandising outlets are out to rip everyone off with extortionate prices. It was my first experience of grub from a disposable Barbie and, it was good and a lot cheaper than the so-called professional outlets. Thanks Tony (I think I still owe you a contribution for that!).

It was a very good nosh up washed down with some beer and we even had enough left over to offer some to the Barnsley fans in the car parked next to us. They were good blokes who travelled from Worcestershire to Barnsley for every match.

It was now time to go into the stadium itself. Once inside, it was deafening – I tried to call Sharon several times but could not hear anything. It was the best stadium DJ or announcer that I'd seen at a football game. He was playing the right songs and tunes and really stoking up the atmosphere in the crowd. You just could not hear yourself think. As mentioned earlier, the colours were a terrific contrast and looked even better as two halves inside Wembley. It differed from the FA Cup final in 1978 as the tickets had gone to the genuine fans this time so although there was only about 75000 compared to 100000 for the Arsenal final, it was split virtually entirely between Barnsley and Ipswich fans. The Cup Final had its usual corporate and affiliated guests there, reducing the actual club support to about 25000 each.

The Play Off final kicked off and it suddenly dawned on me just how critical this game was for not only the club but also the surrounding community. It could be worth millions of pounds to both and was probably now the most critical one off match in Town's history. A passport back to the big time with the feel good factor rubbing off on local shops and businesses and more people having heard of and visiting Ipswich due to their Premiership status.

It was an end-to-end and very entertaining game, albeit difficult to enjoy until Reuser's late goal as there was so much at stake. It was so close to Barnsley equalising when Richard Wright pulled off that outstanding late save from the header and then I will never forget Martin Reuser scoring that magic clinching goal – we were back in the big time at last.

We enjoyed the celebrations for a while at the end but had unfortunately left moments before Reuser came back out onto the hallowed turf complete with blue wig and provided a re-enactment of his goal.

Two main thoughts crossed my mind after the game – a shred of sympathy for the Barnsley fans that had provided great support for their team. You only need to look at the direction they went in following years to realise how narrow the gap is between success and failure.

Secondly, I would like to pass on my thanks to Norwich City. Why you may ask? If they had not won 2-0 at Portman Road in the March, we may well have clinched second place and automatic promotion off Manchester City. Well now we have done it the hard way, winning a trophy at Wembley and going up anyway, this is a far more exciting way to do it and I put it all down to our neighbours from Norwich. Manchester City went up as runners up and did not even get a trophy but we did.

The journey home was like we were floating on cloud nine in a minibus. We saw a group of Reuser supporters that had come over from Holland all dressed in orange (Dutch national team colours) and as we made our way up the A12, people had turned out on some bridges with Town colours as we got nearer to home, although that part of the celebration was small compared to every bridge on the way home from Wembley in 1978.

We got back about eight thirty and Jim, my neighbour from the road behind ours nipped home briefly before calling back en-route for a Chinese take away as a celebration. Just as he arrived, Sky were showing a replay of the highlights – the beers flowed and we relived the glory – I bored Sharon senseless talking her through all the major talking points and moves of the game as they happened and by twenty to ten we were pretty merry. Jim's wife rang up to see where the take away was and was not impressed that it had not been ordered. It was quickly ordered to be ready five minutes after the end of the highlights programme at ten.

When I finally got to bed, the room was spinning (it's amazing what goes into a take away these days!). Shortly after, I was very unwell. I blamed it on the food but Sharon said it was the large quantity of beer drank in a short timescale topping up what we had drunk on and off during the day. I suppose I would have to agree as we have had many take-aways since with no ill affect.

The next day we joined the crowds to acclaim the new Premier League boys doing an open topped bus tour, which my daughter thoroughly enjoyed. Combined with seeing dad go off to Wembley and this celebration, I think that this is where Rachel took her first steps to becoming a fan (the team shirt much earlier must also have helped). She became a fully-fledged Junior Tractor Girl and has been a season ticket holder for a number of years until she went to university this year (2013).

It seemed a long time since Marcus Stewart had pulled us back from the dead in that first leg of the play off semi finals at Bolton when our Premiership hopes had looked to be in tatters.

CHAPTER 9

TRACTOR BOYS BACK IN EUROPE AFTER 20 YEARS

Now moving onto more modern times. This was the era when Town had become known as The Tractor Boys and had had that marvellous first year finishing fifth back in the Premiership in 2000/ 2001. So in 2001/02, they were back in Europe and the draw for the UEFA Cup was eagerly awaited. We came out of the hat against Torpedo Moscow and that was a major disappointment – too far to drive and being one of the world's most terrified fliers, there was no way I would ever be got onto some dodgy Russian airline called Lada Airways or equivalent! Luckily, a great result in Russia saw Town through.

When the next round was drawn, it was against Helsingborg and I really fancied it. It was under two hours on a plane and I thought that I would try and conquer my fears again.

Most of my mates booked flights up without securing a match ticket first. They were more concerned with booking a cheap flight from Stansted than the fact that estimates on the ground capacity for the second leg varied between 7000 – 10000. My mate, Did and I decided to wait until we were sure of our match tickets.

Match tickets sorted so it was down to me to sort out travel. All of a sudden, Mr cheap airline was not any more and £49.99 flights to Malmo were now £249.99. Commercial opportunity to make a killing. I did some more Internet surfing with a map on the lap and realised that Gothenburg was only a 3-hour drive and flights were still available at £39.99. I quickly priced up a hire car and saw we could get one for £70 for two days and booked it all up before those prices went up as well. Gary worked for DFDS and got their local office in Helsingborg to sort us out rooms in a hotel there so we were sorted.

We flew out to Gothenburg on the morning of the match and there were quite a few Town fans taking this route and travelling down by train, although a few others were also hiring cars at the airport too.

There was one very drunk Town fan sitting across aisle from me singing "We're going down with the Norwich" in reference to the plane coming into land over the sea off Gothenburg. My anti flying nerves were jingling again but his daughter soon told him to shut up.

We had been speaking to a chap called Rupert who was travelling by himself and was going to get the train down. As he had not booked it, we offered to give him a lift and share the costs – it worked out well for all of us – cut costs and gave him a hassle free journey.

It was a good run down if a bit interesting on the navigation front. The map I had got was worse than a chocolate teapot. It only showed the main roads and although it showed Gothenburg airport, it was not the one we'd flown to, not that we realised that at the time nor that there were even two airports. In the end, until we got out of Gothenburg heading South, Did and Rupert navigated via the position of the sun. I was not sure but it sounded convincing and they looked like they knew what they were doing so I just drove on. My mate Did read the map and gave instructions – that was also entertaining as he has a very broad accent so I sometimes have trouble understanding places in England let alone Sweden!

We got there in the end and happened to be staying in a really plush hotel on the waterfront that the team were also staying in. We sussed that out straight away as we saw John Kerr, one of the directors standing outside as we arrived. Rupert was staying in a different hotel so we made an open arrangement that if he wanted a lift back the next day, he would be in the hotel reception by a certain time.

We met up with our mates who went via Malmo – John, Gary, Tony etc who had arranged the hotel and had a good drinking session during the afternoon, (this was a new experience – Scandinavia and lots of places to drink – time had moved on or maybe we had missed this place 18 years earlier!). Who will ever forget Harry's Bar across the road from the hotel – hundreds of supporters in it, singing and drinking and David Sheepshanks made an appearance (in the days when he was more popular – no fun being a chairman when it all goes wrong though). Radio 5 was even reporting from there.

The game was played in a friendly atmosphere at the lovely little ground up the hill above the port, on the edge of town.

Before the game, this bloke with a West Country accent came up to us and asked us if we wanted any tickets. I made some sarcastic comment about there even being touts in Sweden but he said that he did not want any money, he'd been let down and just had some spare tickets that he was happy to give away.

We later went into the ground and this chap was sitting next to us. Anyway we know the result, a great comeback after Sereni's blunder and Wilnis's famous falling out with Burley after being substituted. Fabian, I thought you were out of order as it was done for the good of the team and it proved the right decision but saying that, it was obvious Burley could never forgive and forget but oh what a player you have become under Big Fat Joe.

We went back to the hotel afterwards, which had filled up with Town supporters who were on their way to get trains or the hydrofoil back to Copenhagen and had heard that the Town players were staying there. The Team bus got back and the players went straight up to their rooms so soon afterwards, the hordes disappeared. About 20 minutes later, most of the squad came down for a quiet drink and wind down. We enjoyed their company until about 3 a.m., although some of the players did retire earlier.

It probably was not that late really as they had only got back from the ground at around midnight.

I was sorry to leave Helsingborg – it was a lovely place that had become blue and white temporarily, taken over by the travelling Tractor Boys and Tractor Girls estimated at some 3000. We had even sent Delia a postcard explaining the joys of European football, which she would not experience with Norwich. I understand several hundred others sent cards too. I bet they did not say, "Wish you were here!"

The next day we had plenty of time as the flight was not till the evening so we chose a scenic route back to the airport via the forests and lakes of Southern and Central Sweden. We spent a lot of the day trying to find a town with an Internet café with no joy to see who The Tractor Boys had in the next round.

We bumped into this West Country chap again at a filling station near the airport who told us that we had got Inter Milan, which was beyond my wildest dreams. (I had always wanted to watch Town play at either the Nou Camp (Barcelona) or the San Siro (The Milans).) This chap said he'd been speaking with Marcus who was really pleased with the draw.

Back at the airport, I said to this chap, based on the accent, was he related to Marcus Stewart and he introduced himself as Laurie, Marcus Stewart's dad (that explained the spare tickets at the game). He was also travelling with his brother Pete, and also Pete's sons who were Marcus Stewart's uncle and cousins respectively.

We got on the flight back to Stansted. After about an hour, an announcement came over the Tannoy "This is your captain speaking, if you look out of the windows you will see the coast line of Holland and Amsterdam – we should be landing at Stansted in about 50 minutes."

A few minutes later, the plane just plummeted without warning – it must have been for just a few seconds but it felt like an eternity and it was difficult to breathe – you really felt out of breath. A stewardess ran past and went into the cockpit – she then came back out crying. Bearing in mind we were only in the second row and could see everything, this was a real confidence booster to someone like me who hates flying – I thought our time was up. Laurie was sitting next to me and knowing my fear, he tried to put my mind at rest by saying to me that it couldn't have been that bad as they had not put the seatbelt sign on. I replied that it might have been so bad that they had not had time – he did not know what to say to my response! The plane had soon righted itself but then did a smaller drop a couple of minutes later. The next thing we knew was we were landing at Stansted at a rate of knots and with such a hard bump the plane bounced sideways by quite a way. There was a half-hearted cheer on the plane as it stopped and we knew we were safe. We had landed in 25 minutes since the pilot had said it would have been at least 50 minutes so something definitely happened. The stewardess was unwilling to talk about it and despite writing to the airline; they also just fobbed me off so my mind was never put to rest. The passengers disembarked and walked silently into the terminal at Stansted. Bearing in mind that this was a plane load of football supporters returning from an away victory, you would have expected some songs and joviality but there was none so that probably indicated how shaken up everyone was.

We swapped phone numbers and e-mail addresses with Laurie who said that him and Pete would like to go to the game in Italy with us as they'd had such a laugh in Sweden.

I had a real conflict going through my mind – the lack of holiday to be able to travel overland to Italy against my absolute fear at the thought of flying again against the dream coming true of having the chance of seeing the Tractor Boys playing at the San Siro.

In the end we went for one of the official tours recognised by the club. I had rang Laurie and e-mailed him several times to tell him what we were opting for but as he had not got back to me, I went ahead and booked it up for me and Did. John and Tony also then booked up but were on a different plane and staying at a different hotel. I had no sooner booked it than Laurie rang me at work and asked for details and said that he would be booking it up with a request to travel with us. He was going to travel with me and Did with Pete, Marcus Stewart's uncle and also Vicky, Marcus's other half. Laurie asked us to keep it very quiet who she was on the trip as other supporters could sometimes be funny depending how Marcus was playing at the time.

We met up at Stansted in the early hours of the Thursday morning but the weather did nothing to calm my nerves! Apparently the area of Northern Italy around Milan near the Alps was notorious for bad fog and today was no exception. The flights were all being delayed and when Laurie rang Marcus up, the fog was so bad he could see virtually no distance out of his hotel bedroom window and the game could be in jeopardy.

It had been mentioned that we might all be able to go out for lunch with Marcus Stewart and also Marcus Bent in Milan as they were injured and ineligible to play respectively. Unfortunately we spent so long on the ground at Stansted with the plane about to take off then not so we would get an extra breakfast on the plane and then we would not. This went on for two hours and it wasn't until nearly lunchtime that we took off.

We were the last plane out although it was one of the quickest so it overtook several on the way south. It did not help my nerves when the stewardess explained that it did not have sufficient navigating equipment to use in fog. What if the fog came back?!

Anyway, it was nearly 5 p.m. by the time we had checked into the hotel – Vicky and Laurie had grabbed a taxi to make a quick dash to catch up with the Marcuses for a few minutes before they had to set off back to the hotel and we missed out on lunch with them.

My mate John had my mobile number so he rang and we arranged to meet up near the Central Station to go out for a lovely Italian meal before heading for the San Siro. (Central Station was very strangely named, as it was nowhere near the actual centre of Milan.)

We then got the metro out to the San Siro (this was terrific value – ticket equivalent of 50 pence and you used it to get through a type of turnstile to get access to the trains – it did not matter how many times the machine stamped it and we used it for the whole two days we were there). (Don't suppose we should of mind you – well we could not speak Italian!)

We got the metro out to the recommended station for the San Siro but when we arrived, found out that it was still a couple of miles away from the Stadium. Buses that looked like army buses had been laid on.

We got to the stadium and went straight in to enjoy our experience and the build up. The surroundings were breathtaking if the seats etc, a little ageing and grubby. It was chaotic inside and I managed to get separated from our group. I thought that I would head for the row and seat number on the ticket only for a steward to tell me that they had abandoned that and we could sit anywhere. I did not fancy the thought of spending the game by myself, let alone the trip back into the centre of Milan afterwards. In a panic, I rang Sharon, my wife back in England to get her to phone John as my mobile was barred from calling directly to John's for some reason in Italy. In the meantime, she could not get through either and I bumped into them again. As it was so loud, we switched our mobiles off so Sharon could not get any of us and did not know we had met up. She did not know until the next day and was not that impressed.

Just before the kick off, I needed the loo and this was the only time in the four hours inside the stadium that I went. When we got back to England, the Green Un (local football paper), the following weekend had this great colour photo, double paged of exactly where we were in the ground, which was amazing that our exact spot was picked out of over 10000 supporters. Unfortunately, it was taken when I was in the loo and there was a gap where I sat for the rest of the night. My mates thought it hilarious and Did said that at least I could see by the gap where I would have sat – all the others were in the photo. It would have made a lovely souvenir!

We enjoyed the game despite the result and the Italian supporters and police were impressed by our fantastic supporters. The Inter fans even came back into the ground to applaud and acknowledge us at the end and the police posed for photos holding Ipswich scarves. A change from earlier when batons and shields were more apparent as a result of their expectation of trouble.

We left the ground and had the long walk back to the metro – no buses on the way back – made you almost relieved that you'd lost, there was no trouble but it did make you wonder "What if?"

We caught the last train out on the metro and had to change a couple of times. We were on the last trains and the stations were closing as we pulled away – it was almost a case of "Will the last person out put the lights out!"

We had a drink back at the hotel to drown our sorrows although it had nevertheless been a fantastic experience.

We met up with John and Tony and the others the next day and did some sightseeing around the centre of Milan the next day. We bumped into Kevin Beattie outside the stunning cathedral and I remember a group of Tractor Boys outside L'Escala, the world famous opera house singing, "Can you hear Pavarotti sing, I can't hear a xxxxxxx thing!" Who could ever accuse the Tractor Boys of not being cultural!

We had another lovely meal although by this time my nerves were getting the better of me about flying and I was quite ill.

We caught the coach back to the airport and met up with Laurie, Pete and Vicky. It looked like Vicky had been spending Marcus's credit card, as there were some extra bags. Nice one Vicky!

The plane was severely delayed as it had gone off to Russia whilst we were in Milan, despite being chartered to the Town tour operators and we did not leave until some five hours late. The flight was uneventful but I was a nervous wreck and quite ill from the experience following the delay. In fact I was so bad that I cancelled a family holiday to Ibiza the following year as I could not face it and drove to Spain for a holiday instead. I have never flown since and don't intend to.

CHAPTER 10

WHY I HATE VILLA PARK

I have been to Villa Park nine or ten times and the majority of times that I have been there, I have had a fairly forgettable experience arise from it. The only positive in fact that I can associate with Villa Park was choosing not to go the week before the FA Cup Final when they lost 0-6. It is a bit sad that this is the best experience I can remember, because even when I saw them win a crucial match there in 1980-81, it all went wrong soon after. I have even experienced a Duran Duran concert, appearing in their home city that was almost drowned out from teenage girls screaming. A forgettable place and my all time least favourite venue.

My first bad experience of Villa Park was in March 1980 when I went with some of the Cockney Blues, Steve and Nigel (see chapter 3 – Trains And Trainers for more on them). We got the train from Euston to Birmingham New Street and then caught the little feeder train out to Witton, the local station for Villa Park.

We came out of Witton Station and into the main road down to the ground when six Villa fans came out of the Witton Arms across the road towards us and surrounded us. Their ringleader said "Who do you support?" and without warning nor previous rehearsal, Steve sensing trouble replied "Well it isn't Villa you xxxxxxs and punched the ringleader who was the biggest one of them all, hard, a split second before he could have hit Steve. This surprised them all and Steve took his opportunity to sprint for it through the gap. Unfortunately, it took us by surprise as well and before I could react another Villa fan head butted me – luckily I stumbled but kept on my feet and in the general mayhem that followed, I followed Steve and ran for it. As their attention was on me, Nigel had already ran for it as well and although they started to chase us, they soon disappeared down a side street when they saw a police van coming down the road. By this time Steve was coming back and jumped out to flag the van down. My face was swelling up and hurting as we told the police what had just happened. By then another squad car had turned up and they insisted on running me down to the hospital to get me checked over. I was not keen but it was so sore, it made sense. I said to Nigel and Steve they could go into the game but they said that they'd stick with me and come to the hospital.

I arrived at the hospital at about two thirty and luckily was seen quite quickly. It was confirmed that I had a hairline fracture of the cheekbone but there was nothing that they could do and it would just have to heal naturally. I had heard enough and we were in a taxi within five minutes of the x-ray results heading back to Villa Park. We missed the opening half an hour of the game. Shortly after the second half had restarted, I saw two of the gang that attacked us and told a policeman in our section. He radioed someone and within a couple of minutes, they had both been arrested. We had to give a statement at a police station after the game but thankfully they admitted it and pleaded guilty so we never appeared in court and I heard from the police after the case that they got lengthy community orders. I don't quite know how it worked as I had expected that I would have to give evidence but I was not even summonsed.

The next visits back to Villa Park were a double appearance within four days in that epic UEFA Cup winning 1980 – 81 season. Firstly, it was the FA Cup Semi final defeat against Manchester City. It could not have been much crueller – we had had our chances to win in normal time despite losing Kevin Beattie with a broken arm and then it went to extra time when Paul Power popped up to get a late, late winner. I was gutted as my dreams of another Wembley final had gone. I had even had my air horn confiscated by your jobs worth Brummy bobby on the way into the Holte End before the game.

After that major setback, Town still had it all to play for on both the league and European fronts and they had a massive match back at Villa Park on the Tuesday night away to Aston Villa who they were competing with to win the title. It was going to be a tough match following that Extra Time disappointment at the weekend but the lads gave it their, all finding that extra strength from somewhere and they beat Villa 2-1. At that time, I was convinced, following that performance of immense character that it had been the title decider and they were all but home and dry as far as the title was concerned. Sadly, with the UEFA Cup games still to play as well and that extra superhuman effort at Villa Park, it appeared to leave them jaded and exhausted and they had a poor last few league games judged against the standards that they had been setting all season and contrived to gift an undeserving Aston Villa the title, despite that victory a few weeks earlier. They so much wanted to show everyone that night at Villa Park and in the short term, they had won the battle but that extra effort cost them the long-term aim of winning the war (the title).

Next on my list of reasons for hating Villa Park was February 1985 and a whole catalogue of disasters occurred that weekend. Originally, I was not scheduled to go to the Town match at Villa that weekend and was going to see "The Secret Diary of Adrian Mole" in the West End with my girlfriend at the time and her friend with the plan to do some shopping beforehand. About a week before we were due to go, we split up so I decided to go to the game, as opposed to the shopping prior to the play at the theatre in the evening.

We drove to Redbridge on the Central Line of the underground and left my car in the car park there. I then headed for Euston and got the train up to Villa. Yet again, it was a poor game and as we were losing and never looked like scoring, I left 10 minutes from the end so I could get the earlier train back to Euston to give me a bit more of a comfortable duration to get back to the West End for the theatre. Unfortunately, a jobs worth railway worker at Birmingham New Street stopped me running for the train as it pulled away so I missed the earlier train. So I ended up having to get the train I would have, had I stayed to the end of the match and I also heard from Town fans arriving back at New Street that we had equalised late on so I had missed our goal as well. That certainly taught me not to leave a game early on the premise that Town would never score in a month of Sundays. Miracles can happen when connected with football and often do.

After the theatre, we got back to the car at Redbridge and it would not start. A breakdown lorry was called out and that then had a puncture on the way home up the M11. The lorry had no tyre on it so by the time a colleague came out and it was replaced, we did not get home until four in the morning. The next day I borrowed my dad's run around to get to hockey and a brick fell off the back of a builders truck and went straight through the windscreen. When I got to the hockey, late on, I got hit in the face with a stick breaking my nose and getting two black eyes. Not the best of weekends starting at Villa Park again!

Fifth on the list was a League Cup away game in 1988 when I went with my mate Nick and his brother in law and father in law to be who lived in Lichfield near Birmingham. We had the pleasure of tickets in the main Villa Stand and got loads of stick as Town were trounced 2-6. It was not an enjoyable experience; mind you it never is at Villa Park.

Sixth on the list was a decision to take my mate Stuart to his first ever Ipswich game as part of his birthday celebrations in March 2001. Stuart lived in Milton Keynes at the time so it was convenient to spend the weekend up there as it was then a relatively short trip from there up to Villa Park. We splashed out on top price seats in the Villa Stand but it was one of the worst games that I have ever seen (cheap seats with an obstructed view so we only saw half the game would have been preferable!). Stuart has not watched Town since and has even turned down freebies from a season ticket – mind you on first impressions, I cannot blame him.

Finally, I was in Birmingham on business (suitably arranged) in December 2001. I had to go to Birmingham during December 2001 so I may as well coincide it with the game so I can watch it with the travel paid for by expenses. I did the work during the day and then had the choice of a slap up Italian meal at a nice restaurant on our customer's tab or go and have a manky hotdog at Villa Park watching an awful match – despite all my previous experiences of Villa Park, you live in hope so me and a couple of colleagues went to the match. Rob, a Villa fan that worked for our customer at the time described it as a match of the partially sighted against the blind (Villa the former, Town the latter) and I had to agree.

I would say that there are very few advantages from not being in the Premiership but the thought of not having to attend a game at Villa Park certainly has to be the biggest. Perhaps now you can understand my dislike of Villa Park.

CHAPTER 11

OTHER FOND MEMORIES AND HIGHLIGHTS

There have been some terrific memories and experiences that I have gained over the years following Ipswich and many of them are covered under earlier chapters in this book. This chapter will cover some of the additional memories of my close to forty years following the Tractor Boys.

12th May 1984 was the day that I was presented with the title of Ipswich Town Superfan. This was a competition that was ran by the club football programme during the 1983-84 season and required someone to nominate you for dedication (or madness) (it all helps) beyond the call of duty when supporting Ipswich Town. There was then a page long article highlighting feats that had been achieved or undertaken to follow the club. A board comprising, players, manager, directors and other supporters, I believe, selected a winner. It was a great honour and I appeared on the pitch before the last home game of the season with Aston Villa (of all clubs – at least it was not at Villa Park – see Chapter 10). I was given a couple of VIP seats and a car park space and then presented with a Pioneer Laser Disc system as my prize but the biggest acclaim was the applause from both sets of supporters. After the match, we met up with

Kenny at a pub in Stratford St Mary to thank him for his help at the previous away game at Manchester United when Shaky's car had gradually died. (See Chapter 5).

I have also been well known for revolving holidays around matches and one famous incident was getting back from the Scandinavian Pre Season Tour 15 minutes before George Burley's Testimonial with Aberdeen (See Chapter 7). Other similar acts of madness were in May 1989 when Sharon, myself, Nick and his wife Helen had booked a cottage for a week in the Lake District at Keswick. Unfortunately, Ipswich were at Brighton on the Saturday that our holiday started (could not get much more of an opposite end of the country) and then they had the last home league match of the season against Blackburn Rovers the following Saturday (annoyingly as Blackburn away would have only been a short drive on the way home from the Lake District). Solved – we left for the Lake District at eight on the Saturday evening once we had got home from Brighton and stayed in the Midlands at Helen's parents so we arrived at the cottage a day late. We then left at the Lake District at six on the Saturday morning to get back in time for the game against Blackburn the following Saturday. Other holidays have also been cut short (2003/04), Sharon, Rachel and I were staying between York and Scarborough and had to leave early on the Saturday morning to be back in time for the Reading match! Also on more than one occasion we have travelled back early from our regular haunt in North Devon in time for a home game.

The summer of 1992 was another amusing, if not highly annoying memory. We were on holiday in Lyme Regis and Town were due to play at St Austell in a friendly in late July / early August. The details available before we left home all indicated a Friday afternoon kick off which seemed strange, even in the holiday season so I checked with the Ipswich ticket office and they confirmed that it was definitely correct. I was still not convinced and rang Ipswich again on the Friday morning from Lyme Regis, to be told that it was definitely on that Friday afternoon so I talked Neil, Linda and Sharon into a near 300 mile round trip along the coast down to Cornwall. We got to the ground and it looked a bit quiet and the nets were not on the goals. I started to worry at this point and found a groundsman about to mow the pitch. He showed me a poster and it was on the following day, the Saturday! I was gutted and even if we had not been heading home in the opposite direction, would not have fancied that round trip again. I heard when we got home that Town had fielded a strongish side and scored nine or ten the next day so I was even more gutted. I let rip at Ipswich when I got back and they gave me a pair of complimentary tickets for a home League Cup game with Aston Villa, the following December as an apology.

I have also been known for craziness when faced with adversity when it comes to personal injury or disability failing to prevent me getting to games. There was the Charlton Athletic Play Off Semi Final in May 1998 when despite only being discharged from hospital, the day before, I still got to the game at Portman Road on crutches after a knee operation 24 hours earlier.

I also broke my leg and ripped the ligaments in September 2002 on the Wednesday but was still at Portman Road on the Saturday for a home match versus Derby County, the day after I had had a new cast fitted! I say it's dedication, my wife Sharon says it is stupidity. You need to love football to understand.

Another memory was on the golf course at Priory Park, on the banks of the Orwell, next to the old Ipswich airport, in the days when Jason Dozzell played for Town. He was on a tee ahead of us but was on his mobile more than he was swinging his club and he waved us through. Now he was one of my top favourite players over the years so I was really nervous but I needn't have been as I landed the ball on the green about 10 foot from the pin. It was the only one I landed on the green from the tee all day but I could not have selected a better hole to do it on!

A match that has got to stay with me forever was the 1000th match in September 2002 against Norwich City. It was a dream come true that the 1000 were achieved against the auld enemy! As mentioned earlier, I have always been a bit of an anorak and recorded all the games that I had been to so I knew that I was getting close, the previous season when we were still in the Premiership so I was gutted that we would no longer be in the big time when I achieved it. When the fixtures came out, realising that Norwich at home would be the one was the next best thing. Just a pity that I could not see a win rather than the draw. There was an exciting build up and I was interviewed by the East Anglian Daily Times, SGR Radio and then Anglia TV with Donovan Blake and a TV cameraman coming to the house. It might have been me achieving a 1000 games but my daughter Rachel certainly stole the limelight in the interview with her outrageous predictions for the result. I was also lucky enough to obtain Matt Holland's shirt from that game which he has since signed. I have had it framed and it holds pride of place on our study wall.

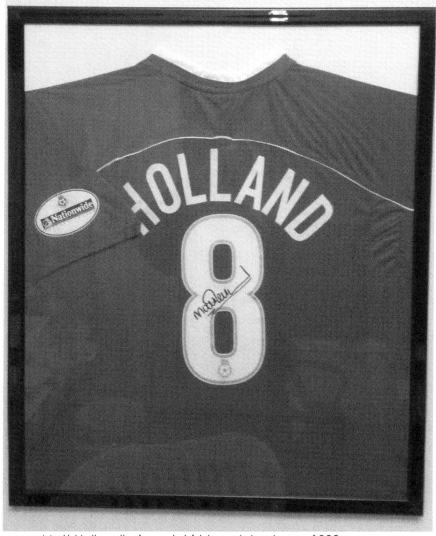

Matt Holland's signed shirt to celebrate my 1000 games v Norwich City

I also always enjoyed the games at Anfield and made a pact that I would go to every match Town played there until they won. I managed 11 games there including travelling up there on a Saturday for a league game we lost 4-0 and then the following Tuesday for a League Cup Semi Final 2nd Leg after we had already lost the home leg. It got to the season we were bottom of the Premiership and relegated and I had had enough and missed my first match there in 16 years and you guessed it, Adam Tanner scored the winner and I had blown my pact! Oh Yea with little faith!

Ipswich Town has also been responsible for some great friendships, various people such as Chris and Nigel from the Cockney Blues that I am still in touch with.

We have also met some lovely families whilst on holiday in the last few years all because I had a Town shirt on. They are John, Bryony, George, Kim and Michaela from Stowmarket and I have since become God Father to their latest addition Charlie. The other family are Alison, Peter, Roo, Matthew and Laura from Bury St Edmunds. Lastly, the Rowsons from Tendring, Mark Theresa Amy and Tom whom we met in the South of France in 2013.

I am also proud to say that my daughter Rachel has become a keen Town Supporter and was a season ticket holder until moving to Canterbury for university. She still manages to come along to several home matches with me each season. Leah, my youngest daughter is now also a season ticket holder taking advantage of the £10 junior season ticket, attending some games each season too – I am not sure if it is the quality football on the pitch or the chance to meet Bluey and Crazee, the mascots, people watching and a large Goody Bag. I'll leave you to make your own mind up!

CHAPTER 12

WHERE IT'S ALL GONE WRONG AND WHAT THE FUTURE MIGHT HOLD

Where did it all go wrong? I'll tell you where it went wrong – finishing fifth in the Premiership and not only qualifying for the UEFA Cup but just missing out on the Champions League on that last Saturday of our first season back in the Premiership up at Derby in May 2001.

If we had just survived or finished in mid table, caution and consolidation would have been upper most in everyone's thoughts for the following season. But no, we were going into Europe and we wanted more and why not – we all jumped on the bandwagon and wanted better the next season. If we are honest we all felt that way, as I am sure, David Sheepshanks did at the time. The difference was he and the other directors had the power that we did not, to spend. Had they not, we would have accused them of a lack of ambition etc, etc so they were in a no win situation.

If we are realistic, fifth was nearly as high as we could ever get in the modern game. We were probably the biggest of all the small clubs with a proven track record of success and financial management over many years even when we were not in the top flight. But realistically, we were never going to do better than the big boys over a whole season. The money on transfers and salaries appeared excessive for a small club to maybe get one place higher the following season but all can see that in hindsight. Mistakes were made but I believe with the best intentions. I think we bought too many foreigners and should have spent more wisely on a couple of established home grown players or at least foreigners that had already proven themselves in the English game. That is where we failed, as they did not have the battling qualities needed to survive in that relegation year.

In the year of relegation, both the board and Burley seemed to spend most of the season denying the inevitable until it was too late. Maybe one gamble in the Transfer market would have made the difference?

Similarly, I felt that the time to have got rid of Burley (and I was a Burley fan) was as soon as we were relegated. Had Royle started the season at Town, he would have got us into at least the Play Offs if not better when you see what they did to Portsmouth and Leicester, the automatic promoted teams that season.

The fan base is amazing – 21000 plus for Walsall or Wimbledon (no disrespect) at home but the club has got to remember that they do not have a god given right to this support and they should appreciate it.

If they are not doing well they need to work harder to fill seats. To this end, the Sales and Marketing Department needs to look at schemes to fill those seats – free seats for school kids, half price for a parent and so on. Once they are in the ground, the catering and souvenirs sells and if it's a good game, they may even want to come back. Bring back free guest passes for season ticket holders, the same applies – the club needs to speculate to accumulate, it's very hard to win new fans but all too easy to lose them. We must never allow the Premiership Shirts to outnumber the Town shirts around the area again.

I am not convinced on Loan Signings – don't get me wrong, some have done us a great service but you can often be in a no win situation – take Kuqi for example, he is at Ipswich for three months and there is a provisional fee agreed at the end of it. If he does really well, surely his club will just up the fee, if he does badly, Town won't want him anyway. The only sensible loans appear to be the Premiership loans to Football League clubs for a whole season to the benefit of the player and the clubs where there is little prospect of a permanent move. These loans from Premiership to Football League Clubs became fewer following the crazy new rule allowing Premiership Clubs to lend to each other – will we end up with Chelsea playing against their own players at various clubs on loan on the run in to the title? The alternative is that a number of players are not allowed to play against a parent club in a crucial match. It beggars belief!

Contracts need to be much more short term and be geared to league and cup success and the league that a player is playing in.

It may also be an idea that the bigger clubs support the smaller clubs financially by contribution to a pot based on annual income and a percentage of any transfer fee over a million. It would be to the big clubs advantage as well as they normally manage to poach a lot of promising players from smaller clubs for ridiculous fees.

On a positive note, violence and hooliganism has reduced significantly in the modern game thanks to CCTV, policing and intelligence gathered. It is now encouraging families to attend again although it is becoming questionable if the ordinary family would be able to afford to attend on a regular basis.

We are where we are due to board decisions, but let's not forget, they were mainly ones that we, the public backed at the time but are now critical of. That combined with the collapse of the Transfer Market and the Television Deals has left the Tractor Boys where they are today.

No matter what I will keep going, being fuelled with great optimism of a quick return to the big time (or maybe it's blind faith).

CHAPTER 13

AND BRINGING US UP TO DATE

And what of The Tractor Boys today – I liked the descriptive term for Ipswich Town originally, hence the title of the book but I am now tiring of it and even believe it goes with too nice and friendly an image of the club. Maybe we need to rethink and become tougher and harder to beat.

A lot has gone on in the last few seasons with Marcus Evans taking over and giving Jim Magilton a chance at the start. In fact we were not far off the playoffs but did not make it under Jim.

Marcus Evans brought in Roy Keane who was a hero of mine when he was a player so I was very pleased with the appointment. But oh boy, little did I know. My and others incorrect assumptions were that Roy would have built up a reputation and contacts in the game and would attract some great players to lift us up the league. I think Roy made a lot of acquaintances who all went in the opposite direction if ever they saw him coming or calling them. The one memory Roy left us was the League Cup Semi Final against Arsenal – that was fantastic and we had won the first leg in front of a sell out when Cesc Fabregas reckoned we played like a rugby team – yes Cesc, we would really play the Gunners off the park trying to play you at an attractive passing game. Anyway lots of renditions of "Swing Low Cesc Fabregas" in the 2nd leg at the Emirates when around 10000 Town fans traveled down. By then Roy had gone and a certain Mr Jewell was hovering in the wings. Mr Fabregas had the last laugh because although we held out till around the hour, we lost 3-0 and 3-1 on aggregate. A new era was about to begin and Roy Keane had gone from hero to zero in my estimation.

Now Paul Jewell was a different kettle of fish altogether, I was never keen (excuse the pun) on his appointment. Yes, he had done well at some of his previous clubs, particularly Wigan, but he had been out of the game for quite a while and I was concerned he had out of date ideas and contacts. He was an amiable almost cheeky scouser that had one thing in common; they both made excuse after excuse that Ipswich was located in the wrong part of the country and they could not attract the players they wanted. Well Marcus Evans backed them well and spent heavily but with no joy. So then did they buy lots of second choice players at inflated prices? It doesn't quite add up when you revisit this period does it?

Now Mick McCarthy has come in and virtually achieved a miracle in 2012/13 when he turned us from relegation certainties with the team he inherited from Jewell in the November to being mathematically safe from relegation going into the last day. Thanks for sparing us that unbearable tension on the last day Mick.

He has steadied the ship and reduced the number of loan players albeit with a small squad. This some including Mick says is an advantage with a more united team spirit. We appear a bit more solid than the last few seasons and build from the back – if we reduce the number of goals we were shipping we were a lot less likely to lose. We have the nucleus of a side that could challenge in Chambers,

Berra, Smith, Cresswell, McGoldrick and Murphy. We also have some promising younger players in Mings, Hewitt and possibly Marriott if he can step up.

I cannot afford the money nor the time to attend the number of away games I used to but I remain a season ticket holder, as does my youngest daughter and try and manage around half a dozen away games still.

Memorable games this season (2013/14) include a weekend after Christmas celebrating my 50th birthday to take in the Bournemouth game where we bumped into the squad having a pre match walk along the cliff tops and also Mick Mills further into town too.

Leah, David McGoldrick and self on Bournemouth seafront

Rachel and Mick McCarthy as team bus arrives at
Bournemouth ground

Other ones were the Leeds Utd game on a Tuesday night in late January enjoying corporate hospitality on an extension of my birthday celebrations.

Yeovil was another must attend game but yet another long Tuesday night away trip. This involved heading into the office to start at 7am and not getting home until 2.30am the following day but a great night with well over 1000 other hardy souls making the trip to visit a lovely little club who made us really welcome. It is a shame they have just been relegated.

Aaron Cresswell with Gaz and self outside Yeovil's ground

The last away game in 2013/14 was taking advantage of Groupon deal offering corporate hospitality at a bargain £42 for the Blackburn Rovers away game – a brilliant day out apart from the match itself.

The faith lives on and I believe with a few tweaks and if we can keep hold of Mick McCarthy and our better players, we could be challenging for the playoffs or better sooner rather than later.

6477676R00085

Printed in Great Britain
by Amazon.co.uk, Ltd.,
Marston Gate.